BUTTERFLY IN THE RAIN

BUTTERFLY IN THE RAIN

The 1927 Abduction and Murder of Marion Parker

James L. Neibaur

ROWMAN & LITTLEFIELD
Lanham • Boulder • New York • London

Published by Rowman & Littlefield
A wholly owned subsidiary of The Rowman & Littlefield Publishing Group, Inc.
4501 Forbes Boulevard, Suite 200, Lanham, Maryland 20706
www.rowman.com

Unit A, Whitacre Mews, 26-34 Stannary Street, London SE11 4AB

British Library Cataloguing in Publication Information Available

Library of Congress Cataloging-in-Publication Data

Names: Neibaur, James L., 1958– | Parker, Marion, 1915–
Title: Butterfly in the rain : the 1927 abduction and murder of Marion Parker / James L. Neibaur.
Description: Lanham : Rowman & Littlefield, 2016. | Includes bibliographical references and index.
Identifiers: LCCN 2015030316| ISBN 9781442251199 (cloth : alk. paper) | ISBN 9781442251205 (electronic)
Subjects: LCSH: Parker, Marion, 1915– | Kidnapping—California—Los Angeles—Case study. | Murder—California—Los Angeles—Case study. | Insanity (Law) —California—Los Angeles—Case study.
Classification: LCC HV6603.P37 N45 2016 | DDC 364.152/3092—dc23 LC record available at http://lccn.loc.gov/2015030316

♾ ™ The paper used in this publication meets the minimum requirements of American National Standard for Information Sciences Permanence of Paper for Printed Library Materials, ANSI/NISO Z39.48-1992.

Printed in the United States of America

CONTENTS

AUTHOR'S PREFACE

The genre of True Crime books investigates crimes that are usually sensational, tell a story, and have an element of suspense, interesting characters, and a satisfying conclusion. This book has all of these. But the way in which I came onto such a project is a story unto itself.

I had been writing books on pop culture history for decades. My specialty was film history. I was researching a project on the silent era when I was distracted by headlines on a microfilm copy of the *New York Times* that told of a twelve-year-old girl who had been kidnapped and held for ransom. There was a picture of the little girl and of her mother, her father, and her twin sister. Initially, my interest was casual. I wondered if they ever found the child—if she had been returned safely for ransom or if perhaps she was rescued and her kidnapper brought to justice. So as I continued to research my own project, I discovered subsequent articles on this case indicating that when the ransom was paid, the child's body was dropped out of an automobile in a sack containing only her head and torso. Her father's screams pierced through the dark Los Angeles night.

Naturally, I was shocked by these events and wondered if they ever identified the killer. Once I saw that had happened, I wondered if he was caught. Then I wondered about his ultimate fate. I realized that if this story was compelling enough as a series of newspaper articles to distract me while busily at work on another project that should have had my entire focus, it might interest others. Thus, I gathered research and put together the book that you are now reading.

My research led to actual court documents about the case, graphic depictions by her killer that were documented by the defense team, and access to some photos (a few of which were too gruesome to consider using—frankly, I wish I had not seen them myself). But as disturbing as the more graphic details could be, there continued to be an element to the story that remained compelling. The entire trajectory of events played out like a suspense drama. The characters had the sort of depth that well-drawn characters in popular fiction might have. Writer friends with whom I discussed this project would frequently say, "Y'know, this sounds like it would make a good movie."

Perhaps one who writes about movies might perceive a nonfiction True Crime book as if it were a movie. While everything contained herein is real and true, these actual events unfold dramatically, the characters on either side of the law extend beyond any stereotype, and the constant element of suspense (wondering about the child's safety, identifying the killer, hunting for him, capturing him, and bringing him to trial) all combined with the reaction from the child's family, from the killer's family, and from the general public add to the suspense. With each new discovery in my research, I found something else about the case that was interesting, unsettling, remarkable, and sometimes frightening.

Then there is the historical element, the fact that this took place during the Roaring Twenties, when the economy boomed, jazz blared, and the movies captivated and amused. This crime's historical setting made it that much more fascinating.

This is the story of Marion Parker, a typical twelve-year-old girl in the 1920s who was kidnapped, murdered, dismembered, and delivered to her father. Her father, an unassuming banker who had lived his life in a most comfortable and ordinary manner, was hit with the worst tragedy imaginable and had his quiet family life thrust into the spotlight. When it was over, he told the press that they just wanted to get on with their lives. Eventually, they were left alone to do so—but not until after they endured what had once been called the crime of the century.

As we recall and detail the events in this book and examine the case and its outcome, the principals involved will be discussed in detail. When possible, the spoken word has been quoted verbatim. However, when that is not possible, conversations have been reconstructed as closely as possible to the reality based on the various sources listed in the bibliography that document those who spoke and those who heard those words. Any information regarding personality traits, relationships, and so on have been pulled from the various sources listed in the bibliography. The public was riveted by this case; they wanted to know everything they could about all involved, especially the victim and the killer. As a result, a variety of feature stories were written about these people and their backgrounds, and it is these sources that allow for a more thorough description of each.

ACKNOWLEDGMENTS

My thanks to Barb Fellion, Lori Kwiatkowski, Terri Lynch, Katie Carter, Cecilia Rasmussen, Bill Cappello, Ted Okuda, the University of Wisconsin Library, and the Racine Public Library interlibrary loan.

INTRODUCTION

The year was 1927.

Americans were flexing their postwar industrial muscle. They were relaxing with the peace and prosperity that World War I had now afforded them, enjoying jazz and dancing the Charleston, laughing at the antics of Charlie Chaplin, marveling at the excitement of Douglas Fairbanks, thrilling to the stunts of Harold Lloyd, swooning to the romance of Greta Garbo and John Gilbert, and marveling at the technical achievement of Buster Keaton.

It was the year that Charles Lindbergh made his transatlantic flight and into the hearts of a hero-worshipping public. It was also the year that Babe Ruth smacked a record sixty home runs, helping the New York Yankees nab the World Series in an event that is still discussed with semireligious awe among baseball fans, even well after this record has been broken.

Popular music celebrated this happy, carefree time with tunes like *When the Red Red Robin Comes Bob-Bob-Bobbin' Along* and *I'm Looking over a Four Leaf Clover*. Some hit songs even presented the idea of comfort and security, with titles like *Me and My Shadow* and *Someone to Watch over Me*.

The Lost Generation gave us literature during this post–World War I era that offered new and different insights. Ernest Hemingway's *In Our Time*, F. Scott Fitzgerald's *The Great Gatsby*, and other books that have since become classics were enlightening readers throughout the world.

But as Americans prepared to celebrate the Christmas season of 1927, ugly headlines came crashing down in every newspaper in the country. From big cities to small towns, everyone was alerted to the kidnapping of twelve-year-old Marion Parker[1] from the safety of her Los Angeles area school.

We have a habit of glorifying the past, recalling the happy times, and overlooking the sad ones. Individuals generally recall childhood as a time of playful innocence. Memories of one's teenage past are nearly always perceived as equally blissful and never fraught with adolescent angst.

This happens when we remember eras in history as well. Important events will often be crowded out of our collective memories. While certainly acknowledging major events like the stock market crash or the world wars, the past usually consists of happy memories of the music, the cinema, the literature, and other areas of popular culture.

In his autobiography, former child star Jackie Cooper recalls the late 1920s and early 1930s as a time when kidnappers were behind every corner. His star status made him a good target for ransom, and he recalls the limitations that were imposed on his childhood in an effort to ensure his safety. But we don't recall this era for its kidnappings; we remember it for the timeless jazz music, great literature, and the silent movies.

Marion Parker was just another ordinary twelve-year-old girl from the Los Angeles area when she was kidnapped and murdered during this era of happy nostalgia and productivity for the nation. This was not a high-profile kidnapping. The Parkers were ordinary middle-class American citizens. They did not have the celebrity status of Jackie Cooper, which would ordinarily have made this the type of story that would have nabbed front-page copy and netted a bundle in ransom money for the perpetrator.

Only a few years earlier, the Leopold and Loeb case, where a young boy was kidnapped and murdered by two wealthy young men attempting to accomplish what they considered the "perfect crime," achieved worldwide notoriety. The initial reports of the Marion Parker kidnapping looked all too similar. And the similarities would continue as more was learned. It was the era of kidnapping, as Jackie Cooper recalled. And the kidnapping of Marion Parker was enough for a full-scale media alert and a nationwide manhunt despite her not having the status of a motion picture star.

While they may not have been celebrities before losing their daughter to the clutches of a kidnapper, the Parkers certainly became well known afterward. Fame and notoriety were thrust on them. They were forced to deal not only with their personal tragedy in the nationwide spotlight but also with the noisy publicity that now intruded into every aspect of their lives. And suddenly, the seamy underbelly of society was on display to upset the Roaring Twenties.

This was before the Internet, before television, even before talking pictures had eclipsed the cinema of silence. It was newspapers throughout the land letting every American know that twelve-year-old Marion Parker of Los Angeles was missing, in the hands of a kidnapper, and being held for ransom. A nation prayed for her safe return.

One day later, the editors of the nation's newspapers pulled out the large-pica type for front-page headlines announcing that Marion Parker had been murdered. A ransom had been paid, but the child's lifeless body was dumped on the street and met by the agonized screams of her father. The public reacted in horror. Money was donated from a variety of disparate sources as a reward for her killer's capture. The murderer's description was given in the nation's press. A public lusting for revenge subjected innocent men who fit that general description to impulsive beatings.

We know the literature of the 1920s, we still know some of the songs, and we are familiar with the era's biggest movie stars. But so many events that rocked the nation are little more than yellowed newspaper clippings from an era that has long since passed us by. The infamy, the notoriety, and even the details that could give us an insight into our own era have been forgotten.

The kidnapping and murder of Marion Parker have been forgotten, crowded out by time and events. Her case does not conjure up the same notoriety as the Leopold and Loeb case or the Black Dahlia murder from the same era. There is no real way to determine just what events will live on and which ones will fade into obscurity.

This is the story of the abduction and murder of Marion Parker. Any dialogue among the people in this story has been taken from actual testimony and is as accurate as current research will allow. The same holds for any description of the characters, from appearance to likes, dislikes, and personality traits.

The Marion Parker murder may have faded away over the decades to the point where even Los Angeles natives have not heard of it, but we haven't quite learned the lessons that it has taught us. If it is known at all, it is just as another tragedy from another time.

But it was once called the "crime of the century."

CHAPTER I

It was a chilly winter morning in Los Angeles on Thursday, December 15, 1927. But despite the cold winds, both Marion and Marjorie Parker were in a cheerful mood as they walked to the streetcar that took them to school. The twelve-year-old twin girls were excited about an all-school Christmas party that was to take place in the various classrooms that day. There is something about the Christmas season that delights youngsters, and the Parker girls were no exception. The school party, the coming holidays, the time off from school, and the days they would spend enjoying their Christmas presents together swirled about their minds.

The Parker twins were almost always together. They had a brother who was much older and whom both adored, but the special bond that is said to exist between all sets of twins was certainly evident despite having so few similarities outside of their appearance. Marjorie was very much a girl who liked girlie things. But Marion had a slightly rougher edge. Not afraid to get dirty or to get hurt, Marion was what would be considered a tomboy.

Marion had many friends who were girls, especially at school. But on weekends, she only occasionally played with the other girls in the neighborhood. While the girls, including Marjorie, would play with dolls and tea sets, Marion would be enjoying toy trains or sometimes even football with the boys. Yet, despite her tomboyish nature and athletic bravado, Marion was, in other ways, an emotionally delicate child.

Marion didn't like to be away from home for long, especially at night. She would play outside all day and enjoy birthday parties and other daytime activities at the homes of her school friends, but as the evening got dark, she preferred to be at home with her parents. Marion was a popular, friendly girl, but she rarely accepted one of the many invitations she would regularly receive from classmates to attend sleep-overs.

Marion could also be a bit apprehensive around adults, unless they were neighbors or friends of her parents. It wasn't fear, as she could be quite gregarious once comfortable, but a certain level of shyness that was alleviated only with better acquaintance. When around those with whom she was comfortable, Marion appeared confident and engaging. She would strike amusing poses when being photographed, while Marjorie offered little more than a pleasant smile. Marion would tell jokes, dance to music coming from the radio or phonograph, and carry on in a silly, childlike manner with far greater abandon than her more sedate twin sister. Marion would merrily laugh aloud at favorite movie comedians like Harold Lloyd and Buster Keaton or amusing radio programs, while Marjorie would enjoy the antics quietly. As Lloyd would perform one of his daredevil stunts, Marion would delightedly fidget in her seat, while Marjorie sat still, smiling, having just as much fun, but far more sedately than her more demonstrative sister.

Marjorie was her mother's girl. When not in school, she was content to help out around the house, learning cooking and sewing. But Marion spent a lot of time at the First National Trust and Savings Bank, where her father worked as an assistant cashier, curiously looking into the various offices and visiting the various officials or standing out front and watching the tellers work. She was not the type of child who faded into the background. She was easily noticed. There was one worker at the bank who certainly noticed Marion Parker. He noticed her well enough to remember her several months later.

Mrs. Mary Holt was the teacher in charge of registration and attendance at Mount Vernon Junior High School, where the Parker girls attended. When the principal, Cora Freeman, was away, Mrs. Holt took charge as administrator. It was she who made the decisions. Mrs. Holt, from all printed accounts, was notable for following the schoolmarm stereotype quite carefully. She was persnickety about the rule book and refrained from any deviation. She was neat and structured and paid attention to detail. Mrs. Holt was quite strict about student deportment and even more careful about strangers visiting the building and inquiring about the children of whom she was in charge in the principal's absence.

Ms. Freeman was absent on December 15 when a nice-looking young man calmly entered the office around noon as the children in the various classrooms were enjoying their Christmas parties. In 1927, there were no cameras and no locked doors where visitors had to be allowed in by authorized school personnel. Anyone could simply walk in from the street and approach the main office to speak to the principal. It was up to the person in charge to meet each visitor, inquire as to their business, double-check their status, and give or withhold permission.

Based on court transcripts and newspaper accounts, the stranger entered the office and approached Mrs. Holt.[1] The dialogue went something like this: "Excuse me, I need to see the Parker girl." Mrs. Holt did not recognize the man. He was small, slender, and had a friendly face and a relaxed demeanor. A faint smile came across his lips as he continued. Rather than interrogate the gentleman immediately, she listened to what he had to say. "My name is Mr. Cooper," he said. "I work with Mr. Perry Parker at the bank. Mr. Parker has been in an accident and is calling for his daughter." Mrs. Holt was confused. "We have two Parker girls at our school," she said. "He wants the younger one," the man continued. Of course, there really was no younger Parker girl. Mrs. Holt knew that, but the stranger did not. Marion was slightly smaller than Marjorie, however, and was born a few minutes later. The girls would often joke that Marion was the "younger sister."

"Do you mean Marion?"

"Yes, yes ma'am, that is her name."

The stranger didn't know her name. He didn't know she had a sister, much less a twin. He knew only that Perry Parker had a daughter. He knew what she looked like. The stranger's relaxed confidence was so imposing that even the wary Mrs. Holt was relaxed enough to be so off her guard as to foolishly feed him the snippets of information he did not have. Mrs. Holt continued to look at the man carefully. She had been known to question parents as to the identity of people who came to pick up their children, often phoning the parents for verification. But Mrs. Holt felt differently about this attractive, confident, well-mannered young man. His demeanor was so calm; it made even the persnickety Mrs. Holt feel uncharacteristically trusting.

Even during the 1920s when this took place, the idea of a stranger picking a child up from school or offering a child a ride was considered a danger of which all youngsters should be aware. But Mrs. Holt didn't stop to think about that. The basic questions that seemed so natural somehow eluded her. This man was friendly, confident, and poised. He didn't take his eyes off her or appear the least bit nervous. And he did say he worked at the bank with Mr. Parker. She knew where Perry Parker was employed. He even stated that Mrs. Holt could call the bank and check, the faint smile remaining on his lips.

Mrs. Holt didn't think it was necessary to call the bank. She didn't even ask such basic questions as "What kind of an accident?," "How serious is it?," or "Why do you want to alert only one of his daughters?" For some reason, the persnickety schoolmarm was too comfortable to inquire any further. This early event, the catalyst of everything that would eventually happen, balanced completely on the culprit's uncanny ability to keep even the otherwise careful Mrs. Holt relaxed enough to fully trust this complete stranger who entered her office. She instructed her assistant, Miss Britton, to summon Marion from her classroom.

After a short wait, Marion arrived at the office, and the stranger approached her with the same calm, confident demeanor he had displayed thus far. He lightly touched the girl's arm as he spoke to her. He identified himself as someone who worked with her father at the bank. He indicated that Perry Parker had been in an accident and was calling for Marion and that the bank sent him to bring her to him. The child left with the stranger, showing no hesitation. She had been at the bank so often that perhaps she felt a hint of recognition when looking at the man's face. Perhaps, as with Mrs. Holt, she felt the same comfort and safety while looking into his eyes.

This was the 1920s, a time when children trusted adults and authority figures with a certain blind faith. Marion trusted Mrs. Holt's authority just as she had trusted the man who patiently escorted her from the school building and into his waiting car. Mrs. Holt did not ask Marion if she knew or recognized the man. When the stranger left with Marion, Mrs. Holt assumed that all was well. Even when principal Cora Freeman returned to the school and Mrs. Holt informed her about Perry Parker's accident and that Marion had been picked up by a family friend, all was assumed well. Trusting Mrs. Holt's authority and professionalism and being fully aware of her careful nature, Mrs. Freeman refrained from asking any of the standard questions as to the severity of the accident or why Marjorie was not alerted as well. No more was thought about it. And, perhaps even more curiously, nobody thought it necessary to tell Marjorie anything.

Marjorie Parker waited for her sister outside of the building after school. They always met up after classes ended and went to the streetcar together. She waited a long time and could not get back into the building to find Marion, who she concluded was likely helping out in one of the classrooms. She had done that before and came out late enough where both girls had to run to catch the streetcar home. This time, Marion never came out, and Marjorie did not want to miss the streetcar, so she ventured on alone.

When Marjorie arrived home without her sister and told her parents that Marion did not meet her after school, the Parkers were not initially alarmed. It was likely that there was a simple reason. They also reasoned, as Marjorie had concluded, that Marion stayed a bit too long in the classroom helping the teacher clean up after the Christmas party and lost track of time. She could be arriving on a later streetcar. Children often don't think to watch the time and don't think to phone home. The Parkers felt they had no reason to worry, so their minds did not even venture toward the possibility of anything having gone wrong. Still, Perry Parker called the school's office. It was getting late and would be dark soon. Perry Parker knew that Marion didn't like being away from home as it got dark and probably didn't realize how late it was getting. So he felt it would be a good idea to simply drive over to the school and pick her up himself. He phoned the number that would connect him to the main office. Mrs. Holt answered the phone. Perry Parker greeted her and identified himself.

According to court transcripts and newspaper accounts, Mrs. Holt was shocked to hear from Perry Parker and asked how he was feeling.[2] "I feel fine, Mrs. Holt," he said. "Thank you for asking." Of course, Mr. Parker was responding as if Mrs. Holt was exhibiting a generally kind greeting, and he responded the same way. He continued his inquiry. "Is Marion still at school? She didn't arrive home with her sister, and I was preparing to drive over and pick her up."

Mrs. Holt asked if she had come home with "the man you sent to pick her up." Mr. Parker was confused. Mrs. Holt explained the situation. A cold feeling went through Perry Parker as he was told of the family friend, the accident, and Marion's departure from school hours before. Parker's friendly demeanor turned to anger mixed with concern.

"I was not in any accident and did not send anyone to pick Marion up from school!"

Perry Parker had been home the entire day. He took the day off to spend with his wife. It was his fortieth birthday.

CHAPTER 2

Perry Parker and his wife, Geraldine, immediately became very worried. They had seen the headlines about kidnappings that were taking place for ransom demands. The Parkers were among those who, only a few short years before, had read in shocked horror of the Leopold and Loeb kidnapping case that left a young child dead. Often when worry turns to panic, one's imagination reaches for the most horrible of possibilities. With so many frightening possibilities swirling in his head, Perry Parker decided to call the police.

Just as Parker was preparing to phone and report Marion's absence, his doorbell rang. Hanging up the phone before placing his call, Parker went to the door to find a Western Union telegram, sent from Pasadena. It stated, "Do positively nothing till you receive special delivery letter." Marion appeared to have signed it, although it did not seem likely that these were her words. Parker followed orders, doing nothing until he received another telegram a short time later. The waiting was horrible, but he felt that he had better heed the first telegram's warning. The second telegram was from Alhambra, California. "Marion secure. Use good judgment. Interference with my plans dangerous." It was signed "George Fox," a name that nobody in the family recognized.

Marjorie Parker told her parents that she recalled a man in a gray coupe driving alongside the streetcar on which she and Marion were riding to school. He tried to get their attention and gestured as if he wanted them to get off the streetcar and come with him. Being generally wary of strangers and, like most youngsters of any era, told by their parents never to get in a car with anyone they didn't know, they simply ignored the strange man. Marjorie thought nothing more of this until the telegrams started coming in, and the Parkers realized their child was in the hands of a kidnapper.

It is not known if Marion recognized the man with whom she left school as the same man she and her sister saw in the gray coupe. If so, one wonders why she didn't refer to that incident, which would have been only a few hours old. But again, this man was in the presence of trusted authority figures. Mrs. Holt introduced him. Marion was comfortable with the situation when surrounded by so trusted an adult as her school's assistant principal.

Night became morning, and a sleepless Perry Parker wrestled with the conflict of wanting to contact the police about his beloved daughter and warnings from her kidnapper not to do so. He paced the floor, weighed all of his options, and was haunted by a series of "what-ifs." Was Marion being hurt? Being attacked in any way? Was she only frightened, or was she also undergoing any one of a number of hideous possibilities? All of these thoughts consumed Parker's mind. Finally, he could stand to wait no longer. He phoned the police, and they quickly arrived to question the family so they could begin to search for Marion.

In this era of kidnapping, Marion Parker was not the only missing child on the roster of the Los Angeles police force. At the time Parker phoned and reported Marion's ordeal, the police had already received five other missing-children reports. Fifteen-year-old Robert Leslie had been missing since leaving for school the morning of December 7. However, it was reported that he had announced he was leaving home, never to return. Thus, police suspected that Robert Leslie was far more likely a runaway rather than a kidnap victim. There was also twelve-year-old Hazel Warner, who had not been seen since Thursday afternoon. According to her mother, Hazel phoned that she was on her way home once her afternoon music lesson had ended. She never arrived. Seventeen-year-old Lillian Runyon left home with, according to her mother, "a strange young man in a dark coupe" on December 10. Police wondered if this was the same coupe Marion and Marjorie had seen from the streetcar and if it was the same man who abducted Marion from school. Was the Runyon girl in on it? Was she another in a series of victims who also included Marion? These were not likely conclusions, but every possibility had to be considered.

The police happened to be with the Parker family, taking statements from each of them, when a special delivery letter arrived on Friday morning, having been mailed at 6:00 p.m. Thursday evening. It stated,

> P.M. Parker:
> Use good judgment. You are the loser. Do this. Secure seventy-five $20 gold certificates U.S. Currency 1500 dollars at once. Keep them on your person. Go about your daily business as usual. Leave out police and detectives. Make no public notice. Keep this affair private. Make no search. Fulfilling these terms with the transfer of currency will secure the return of the girl. Failure to comply with these requests means no one will ever see the girl again except the angels in heaven. The affair must end one way or the other within 3 days. 72 hours. You will receive further notice. But the terms remain the same.
> Fate.

What was even more chilling was an accompanying letter written in Marion's own hand:

> Dear Daddy and Mother:
> I wish I could come home. I think I'll die if I have to be like this much longer. Won't someone tell me why this had to happen to me? Daddy please do what this man tells you or he'll kill me if you don't.
> Marion Parker

Of course, Parker had already contacted the police. But fearing for his daughter's safety, he made a deal with the officers and detectives to keep the investigation away from the press, hoping for the possibility of a successful ransom exchange. Decades before the Internet or intrusive reporters from twenty-four-hour cable television newscasts, it was much easier to keep things quietly withheld from the media, at least for a time.

The police were baffled by the ransom demand of only $1,500. This was a fair amount of money in 1927, of course, but certainly not at the level of a typical ransom demand, which was usually in the area of six figures. Investigators wondered if perhaps the kidnapper had an ulterior motive beyond so paltry a demand as $1,500 ransom, such as revenge. Maybe he realized that the Parkers were not people of means where a large sum would be possible for them. The police could only speculate at this point. The Parkers were carefully interviewed as to all of their friends, coworkers, acquaintances, and relatives. This gave them pause, as they couldn't imagine being targeted by anyone even remotely near their circle. They epitomized the ordinary American family and were without controversy. They couldn't imagine anyone wanting to kidnap one of their children for ransom. But the detectives had to examine every possibility, no matter how remote, and give it, at least, marginal consideration.

Perry Parker didn't waste time pondering what to do. He immediately drew the requested ransom money out of his personal account at the bank, collecting $1,500 in $20 bills. He did, however, have the presence of mind to record the serial number for each bill, which numbered K68016901 to K68016975, inclusive. His instinct as a banker served him well in this instance.

Following the instructions of the kidnapper, Perry Parker worked a regular day at the bank as if nothing was wrong. He fought hard to keep his nerves in check, going about his business in as relaxed a manner as he possibly could. He didn't need anyone to notice he was not himself. He didn't need to field questions as to whether anything was bothering him. Fortunately, everyone was busy enough with his or her own responsibilities. Parker did a good job of keeping his troubles to himself. He was glad that no friendly coworkers casually asked him how his family was doing. And Marion, a frequent visitor to the bank, was not mentioned either. It was very difficult, but Perry Parker made it through the workday without tipping anyone off. He even felt that because of his consistent cooperation, perhaps the kidnapper would be pleased enough to let his daughter go without harming her.

While Parker spent the day at the bank, the police were at Mount Vernon Junior High School questioning Mary Holt. She gave them a description of the kidnapper as being twenty-five to thirty years of age, five feet eight inches in height, and 150 pounds; having a slender build and thin features; being smooth shaven; and having a medium complexion and dark brown, wavy hair, with the appearance of having been waxed. Mrs. Holt said he was a man who speaks very good English and is apparently well educated and who was wearing a brownish-gray herringbone overcoat and a dark gray hat. Her observation was very keen and her attention to detail very helpful. But she was so shattered on finding out that Marion had been placed in the hands of a kidnapper due to her lax attitude that she suffered a breakdown and had to sleep under sedation. The police were relieved that she was lucid enough to offer so many significant details in her frazzled condition.

When Parker returned home from work late Friday afternoon, there had been no further word from Marion or the kidnapper. Then, at 8:00 p.m., the phone rang. Perry Parker was met by a male voice on the line.

"Mr. Parker, do you have the money?"

The voice seemed calm, not angry and not even dangerous.

"Yes, I have. Is Marion all right?"

Parker tried to sound calm as well despite the panic he felt inside.

"I'll call back in five minutes."

It wasn't five minutes. It wasn't even fifteen minutes. Twenty minutes slowly ticked by while Parker waited by the phone, his nerves shattered. He wondered what Marion meant in her letter when she stated, "I think I'll die if I have to be like this much longer." Be like what? Was she tied or restrained? Was she experiencing any pain or discomfort? What unspeakable things could this man be doing to her? Was he alone, or were there others?

There were some things Perry Parker didn't allow himself to think about in much detail. They were too horrible to imagine. He just wanted her home and safe as quickly as possible. Whatever might have happened to her could be dealt with once she was back in the comfort of her home and family. Parker's imagination was running wild. He tried to ignore it and concentrate on what needed to be done before she could return. The kidnapper still hadn't called. Finally, the phone rang again. It had been a full thirty minutes since the previous contact.

"Listen to me carefully, Mr. Parker. Get in your car alone and drive north on Wilton to Tenth and turn to the right one short block to Gramercy and park on Gramercy just north of Tenth."[1]

Parker agreed to do as the kidnapper asked, hoping that after this exchange, his daughter would be safely in his arms. He wanted no interference from the police. He was willing to go anywhere and pay any amount to get his daughter back safely and did not care what happened to the criminal afterward. Vengeance was not on his mind, only his child's safety. He could think about justice later.

Parker took the $1,500 and went to his car, doing exactly as the kidnapper ordered. He drove alone, making sure he adhered to all speed limits so as not to be stopped by the police, who did not realize his situation or his current quest. Once Perry Parker arrived at the designated area, he waited impatiently for a sign from the kidnapper. He sat still and quietly in his car, parked on Gramercy, carefully eyeing every passing vehicle and wondering if it contained his missing daughter and her kidnapper. Hours slowly creeped by. It was 11:45 p.m. when Parker finally realized he was not to be met by anyone. With a heavy heart, he returned home.

On his arrival back at home, Parker was met with the news that Los Angeles police had followed him, hoping to capture the kidnapper. Unfortunately, something must have gone wrong because the kidnapper realized well enough not to make himself known. In their attempt to help, the police inadvertently foiled the exchange. Marion would not be coming home that evening. Parker was furious with the police, and the kidnapper was furious with Parker.

CHAPTER 3

The botched ransom exchange had shaken things up considerably, and finally it was no longer possible to keep the story out of the papers. This was not something that was going to be handled quietly without anyone realizing anything. This was a major crime, it involved a child who might be in danger, and the newspapers were ready to start reporting about it.

On the morning of Saturday, December 17, news of Marion's kidnapping exploded in the nation's press. The era of kidnapping had another story to tell, and it was widely reported in newspapers throughout the country. Nearly every paper offered it on the front page, immediately capturing the public's interest. A child was in danger. She was in the clutches of a kidnapper. Suddenly, the entire nation was on alert.

In the *Los Angeles Times*, Marion was described as being twelve years of age, being four feet six inches in height, and weighing 100 pounds, with brown eyes, an olive complexion, and bobbed hair. When she disappeared, she was wearing an English print dress of mixed colors, brown Oxford sports shoes and stockings, a sweater vest with no collar or lapels with a blue back and blue sleeves, and no hat. A photo of her accompanied the description.[1]

The papers also printed the description of the kidnapper that Mary Holt had provided to police, adding that he was driving a dark-colored coupe or convertible roadster with a spare tire in the rear. The newspapers also contained confident quotes from Chief of Detectives Herman Cline. Cline indicated that Marion's safety was the major concern of the department and that it was only a matter of time before she was returned home and her kidnapper was apprehended. Despite the situation the night before, the Parkers continued to believe in the police. Perhaps in our more modern, more litigious era, the botched Friday night exchange would be blamed on the police choosing to follow Parker and ultimately being spotted by the careful kidnapper, resulting in a series of lawsuits and internal investigations. But the Parker family understood and continued to take comfort in the department's passionate efforts to rescue their daughter and bring her kidnapper to justice.

Herman Cline, nicknamed "Hard-Boiled Herman," was a classic 1920s Los Angeles detective, the type who might have been played by a James Cagney or Edward G. Robinson type of actor during the early 1930s in a Warner Bros. melodrama. Cagney and Robinson were not the prototypes. It was characters like Cline who were to influence the later movie characterizations of actors like these.

A tough-as-nails, no-nonsense sort, Cline would steamroll through a case and typically emerge successful. Taking a keen interest in the plight of a kidnapped little girl, Cline stated that scores of detectives had been relieved of all duties and assigned to the Marion Parker case. He was receiving full cooperation from all detective and police forces throughout the Los Angeles area, including another chief of detectives, George Contreras. Contreras, much like Cline, was a tough guy with a real familiarity with the streets of Los Angeles. The Parkers felt that with two powerhouse detectives like Cline and Contreras on the case, Marion's safety and her kidnapper's capture should be only a matter of time.

Police stated that they still believed that someone close to the Parker family perpetrated the kidnapping in that the kidnapper knew that Parker worked at the bank and that he had a daughter. The Parkers still could not comprehend that as a possibility. They did understand the idea that Marion would more likely have left the school building with an acquaintance than with a stranger but still could not believe that anyone they knew would put their daughter in peril.

Perry Parker was clearly baffled, telling the press, "I can't understand why anyone would wish to hurt us. We live very quietly, and I am sure I have no enemies. We are of moderate means, not the type that would be marked by kidnappers. Marion is just a healthy, normal sort of child. She was full of life and play all the time. All we want, of course, is to get her back safely. Nothing else matters. And I feel that we shall. We haven't given up hope by any means. I have an idea that when her abductor realizes the effort that is being made to find her, he will be frightened and release her. She isn't the type of child that anyone would wish to harm."

Marion's frail mother, Geraldine, was so grief stricken that she could barely talk to reporters. She stated, "Marion will be terribly frightened, but she'll try not to show it. And in spite of her youth I feel that if she has any chance in the world to get word to us she will do it, for she's resourceful and she thinks pretty sensibly. I think she had a little money with her and I'm sure we'll have word from her soon."[2]

As Mrs. Parker spoke, reporters noticed a train and track set on the living room floor. They were told that Marion had put it together a few days before her disappearance. They were leaving it alone as a reminder that she would someday come home to play with it again.

Chief of Detectives Cline continued to insist that Marion would be returned unharmed and that the kidnapper would be caught. He was sure all would be well. Perry Parker continued, "The money means nothing. All I want to know is that Marion is not harmed and to have her sent back to us. The waiting is terrible, and it seems as if time would never pass. Surely we will hear something before the day is over."

The Parkers did indeed hear something. Just as Perry Parker feared, the kidnapper realized that he had been trailed by police and, as a result, did not make the planned exchange Friday night. On Saturday, Parker received another special delivery letter:[3]

P.M. Parker:
When I asked you over the phone to give me your word of honor as a Christian and honest businessman not to try a trap or tip the police you didn't answer. Why? because those two closed cars carefully followed your car north on Wilton to 10th and stopped shortly off Wilton and proceeded to circle the block on Gramercy, San Marino, Wilton, and 10th. I knew and you knew. What for? Mr. Parker I am ashamed of you! You'll never know how you disappointed your daughter. She was so eager to know that it would only be a short while before she would be free from my terrible torture and then you mess the whole damn affair. How can the newspapers get all these family and private pictures unless you give them to them? All this continues after you received my strict warnings. Today is the last

day. I mean Saturday December 17th, 1927. I have cut the time to two days and only one more time will I phone you. If by 8 p.m. today, you have not received my call then hold a quiet funeral service at your cemetery without the body on Sunday the 18th. When I call I'll tell you where to go and how to go. So if you go don't have your friends following. Pray to God for forgiveness for your mistake last night. If you don't come in this good, clean, honest way and be square with me—that's all!
Fate—Fox

Another note, written in Marion's own handwriting, was included with the kidnapper's angry tirade. It did nothing to calm Perry Parker's fears. But it did make him even more anxious to make the ransom exchange and get his daughter home safely. Parker recognized Marion's handwriting as he had with her previous note. He had no problem believing that these notes were actually written by her, even if they were not composed by her:

Dear Daddy and Mother:
Daddy, please don't bring anyone with you today. I'm sorry for what happened last night. We drove right by the house and I cried all the time last night. If you don't meet us this morning you'll never see me again.
Love to all,
Marion Parker
PS: Please Daddy; I want to come home this morning. This is your last chance. Be sure and come by yourself or you won't see me again.
Marion[4]

Perry Parker was now frantic with worry and contacted Chief of Detectives Cline personally, insisting that he be allowed to act alone. He did not want another botched delivery to result in his daughter being killed or even hurt. Being a simple, hardworking family man with no conflicts in life, Parker was new to this sort of a situation, and he didn't quite know what might be best. So he had to now rely on a gut reaction.

Herman Cline was skeptical about allowing Parker to go alone to meet the kidnapper. However, he understood the father's concern. He realized that this was something Parker needed to do. The detective relaxed his tough demeanor and gave Parker his wish.

Parker received two more letters from "Fox" before receiving any phone calls. These appeared less angry and gave the worried father some hope that this nightmarish ordeal may soon be over:

> P.M. Parker:
> Please recover your senses. I want your money rather than to kill your child. But so far you have given me no other alternative. Of course you want your child, but you'll never get her by notifying the police and causing all this publicity. I feel however that you started the search before you received my warning, so I am not blaming you for the bad beginning. Be sensible and use good judgment. You can't deal with a master mind like a common crook or kidnapper.
> Fox—Fate.

Another letter arrived shortly thereafter, emphasizing the same points. It appeared that the kidnapper wanted an end to this situation as desperately as the others:

> P.M. Parker:
> Fox is my name. Very sly you know. Set no traps. I'll watch for them. Get this straight! Remember that life hangs by a thread. I have a Gillette ready and am able to handle the situation.
> Fate

As afternoon fell into evening, Parker's phone rang. It was the now familiar voice giving Perry Parker one more chance to make the exchange of the ransom money for his daughter. "If you fail, Marion will die," the voice stated, immediately after which the line went dead. Perry Parker was worried but determined. He was not concerned about putting himself in danger. He was willing to make whatever sacrifice necessary to rescue his daughter from the clutches of this kidnapper. In his thoughts, Parker wondered, "What if all he wants is money?" If that is the case, the money means nothing as long as Marion is safe.

The kidnapper was upset about the failure to make an exchange the night before. He was angry about the newspapers offering Marion's picture and the kidnapper's description. His note referred to "terrible torture." What could that be? Parker did not allow his imagination to wonder too much about that. He knew his daughter was alive. He wanted her to stay that way. He wanted her home. Then he could consider justice and vengeance as well as what would be necessary to help Marion get past whatever ordeal she was enduring at the hands of the kidnapper.

Parker did not hear from the kidnapper again until 7:15 that evening. He was asked to leave immediately and drive north on Wilton Place to Fifth Street. He was told to turn right at the intersection, drive another three blocks east, and park at the corner of Manhattan Place. Perry Parker carefully wrote down the kidnapper's instructions. He had the money ready. He had the cops agreeing to stay away. He was ready to make the exchange and determined to not let anything else hamper it. The police were on alert but did give Parker their word that they would make no attempt to follow him. He then asked the kidnapper how he would know him. The kidnapper stated that he would recognize Parker's car. It was time to try again.

CHAPTER 4

Nervous and concerned for his daughter's safety, Perry Parker carefully made the journey according to the kidnapper's instructions, which he had written down. Again, he had the $1,500 in $20 bills, ready to exchange them for his daughter's safe return. This time, the police would not follow him. He was acting alone as per the kidnapper's wishes. The police were concerned that Parker was stumbling into a trap. Parker didn't care to think about such a possibility. He wanted his daughter back safely and didn't want another botched exchange to result in her death.

Once he arrived at the destination, Parker sat quietly in his car, just as he had during the first, abortive attempt to make the same exchange. He hoped he did not have to wait a long time, as each minute seemed like an eternity. While waiting, he thought about the condition Marion might be in. If she was harmed or underwent trauma of any kind, he believed a doctor's care and the safety of her home and family was all she would need. He tried not to let his mind wander, but the very act of waiting in the Los Angeles night forced his imagination into high gear. The street was dark, with little activity. This stillness added to his tension. Parker's nervous imagination tried to block out the possibility of Marion having been assaulted in any way.

It was just after 8:00 p.m., when Parker saw a car's headlights approaching from his rearview mirror. At first, he was worried it might be Chief Cline, Chief Contreras, or perhaps any random police car assigned to remain nearby and keep an eye on things. Of course, such an action would probably botch the entire deal. Parker realized he was wrong when the car pulled up next to his. The driver leaned out of the window, a bandanna covering the lower part of his face. He slowly raised a sawed-off shotgun and pointed it at Parker.

"You see this gun?"

Despite the bandanna, the muffled voice was familiar to Perry Parker from the telephoned warnings.

"I see it."

Parker tried to keep the tone of his voice calm. So did the kidnapper.

"Did you bring the money?"

Perry Parker pulled the $1,500 from his pocket and showed it to the man peering at him from the other car—the kidnapper's cold eyes seeming even more intense with the bandanna obstructing the rest of his face.

The kidnapper demanded, "Give it to me!" But Parker wanted to see Marion first. He had gotten this far and was not interested in taking any chances.

"Where is my daughter?"

The kidnapper revealed the girl next to him, wrapped in a blanket. Parker could just barely see her face in the darkness, and he recognized it as his missing daughter. She appeared to be in a daze, looking straight ahead with little reaction. Parker began calling to her but was stopped by the kidnapper, who said she was asleep. Despite the darkness, Parker could tell Marion's eyes were open. He figured she was likely drugged. No time to think about that now. He just wanted his daughter back in his arms. He would worry about her physical condition later.

Parker slowly held his arm out the window, passing the money to the kidnapper. The kidnapper reached across Marion and stretched his arm out the passenger-side window, with the shotgun aimed at Parker the entire time. The kidnapper took the money. There was an awkward pause as the kidnapper inspected the ransom, making sure all was there. Satisfied, he leaned toward the window and faced Parker.

"Wait here just a minute," the kidnapper ordered.

The kidnapper leaned back and disappeared into the darkness of his car. The car was put into gear and slowly moved forward. Perry Parker watched carefully as the car containing Marion came to a stop. The passenger door opened, and an object fell to the curb. The car drove off quickly, and Perry Parker slowly drove his car forward and concentrated on the object that had been thrown to the curb. He parked his car, leaped out, and looked down at the bundle lying near the gutter. He saw his daughter's face peering out of a wrapped blanket. Kneeling beside the bundle, he reached down and lifted it toward him, throwing his arms around his 100-pound daughter, and pulled her closely toward him. He noticed the package was suspiciously light.

"Marion?"

Her eyes were indeed open, but she offered no response.

"Marion?"

The bundle seemed small. Perhaps her knees were bent?

"Marion?"

His hands trembling, Parker furiously undid the blanket to reveal his daughter. As he pulled away the last corner, he saw that it contained only her head and torso down to about the navel. The legs were gone. The arms were severed at the elbows. Her open eyes stared blankly, straight ahead and showing no recognition or sign of life.

Perry Parker's agonized shrieks rang through the dark night. They alerted nearby merchants who came out and comforted him, while others ran back into their places of business and phoned the police. Detective George Contreras was among the first of the officers to arrive, maybe seven minutes later. Perry Parker was, by then, standing in shock by his automobile surrounded by well-meaning citizens trying in vain to comfort him. Grown men were in tears, but Parker was too stunned to cry. Contreras approached the ashen-faced father and gently asked, "Where is she, Mr. Parker?" "She's over there," Parker said, pointing to the body. "God bless her little heart." And then he broke down into sobs, collapsing in the arms of two men who were standing near him.

Contreras approached Marion's body and saw that it was not complete. He noticed that her eyes were open and looked more carefully at her face under the glare of the streetlight. The eyes had been stitched open with a needle and thread. Makeup had been applied to her cheeks to give the illusion of life in the dark night. Contreras's hard edge dropped as he felt a pang of sickness. Tears welled up in his eyes. Parker was taken from the scene by police and brought home. Another officer followed behind, driving Parker's car. Once home, Perry Parker had to tell his wife, son, and other daughter that Marion was dead.[1] He did not offer details; those he would share privately only with his son.

Marion's body was taken to the morgue to be examined by Dr. A. F. Wagner, a neighbor of the Parkers who knew the family well. He was brokenhearted as he accepted the body for examination. Pictures were taken of her remains.

Word quickly got back to police headquarters that Marion Parker was dead. Officers throughout the area began a search for the kidnapper's vehicle based on a description by Perry Parker. On hearing of Marion's death and the details surrounding the state of her remains, even the strong, unflappable "Hard-Boiled" Herman Cline put his face in his hands and wept.

Meanwhile, the kidnapper had traveled far from the site where he had deposited Marion's body and dropped off his car at Ninth and Grand. He decided to get a bite to eat at a café on Broadway between Fifth and Sixth streets. He paid for his meal with one of the $20 gold certificates Parker had just given him as ransom for his daughter. Carrying new money and feeling confident that he had committed the major crime that had been his goal, the kidnapper flashed his confident smirk at the café's pretty, young cashier. "You would be surprised if you knew who I was," he said, and wandered back out into the dark California night.

CHAPTER 5

Dr. A. F. Wagner performed the autopsy on Marion's remains shortly after 9:00 p.m. Saturday night. He stated that it was one of the most difficult postmortem examinations he ever had to perform since he had been living next door to the Parkers for the past four years and knew the family very well.

While examining the parts of the body that had been recovered by police, the doctor noted how it consisted of only the head, the trunk down to an inch below the navel, and the upper arms intact but the forearms removed at the elbows. He discovered there was also a two-and-a-half-inch cut made by a knife on top of the left shoulder. He found no other marks on the body, no discoloration of the face from bruising or asphyxiation, and no contusions about the neck.

Dr. Wagner also noticed that the eyelids were stitched open. The lungs, heart, trachea, stomach, liver, and kidneys were all intact and in healthy shape without any evidence of contusion. A towel was stuffed into Marion's abdominal cavity, as was part of a man's shirt. The police used these in hopes of possibly being led to the killer through any fingerprints or other tangible evidence.

While Dr. Wagner performed the autopsy on the recovered portion of Marion's body, the police had located the kidnapper's Chrysler coupe. The parking lot attendant stated that the driver was "a young dark-haired man" who said that he would pick up the automobile on the following day. Detectives were stationed in a stakeout nearby, waiting for the kidnapper to show up on Sunday for his car.

Sunday morning's headlines exploded throughout the nation. Some newspapers carried a boxed-in statement, almost like an advertisement, that alerted readers to the event, the efforts of the police, and a description of the killer:[1] "Staggering to the imagination, abhorrent to every human instinct," she had been

> subjected by her kidnapper to unknown and unnamable horrors, slain, dismembered, and—as a crowning, frightful touch to the hell-born scheme of a fiend incarnate—the pitiful fragments of her hacked-up body wrought into the ghastly guise of a living child and delivered to her father. . . .
>
> The Police are doing everything possible to apprehend this fiendish slayer, but this is not a job for the police alone. Every citizen of Los Angeles, every resident of the Southwest, must assist. If every pair of eyes within the area of the murderer's possible movements is vigilantly alert . . . his chances to elude the gallows will be scant indeed.
>
> THE MURDERER: American; 25 to 30 years of age; five feet eight inches in height; 150 pounds; slender build; thin features, smooth shaven; medium complexion; dark brown hair, wave and has appearance of being waxed; speaks good English and is apparently well educated. Sometimes wears brownish-gray herringbone overcoat and dark gray hat.
>
> THE MONEY: He has in his possession seventy-five $20 United States gold certificates, serial numbers K68016901 to K68016975, inclusive. Merchandise and businessmen are requested to keep a memorandum of these numbers and to paste the numbers on their cash registers. If any of these bills are presented, notify the police detective bureau, Metropolitan 6100, immediately.

The Roaring Twenties, the Jazz Age, the heyday of the silent movie, the postwar period of brilliant American literature, the Charleston—the era of kidnapping.

America read in collective shock the gruesome details presented by the newspapers. Referring to Marion's corpse as a "hacked-up body" is gruesome for any era, much less the carefree 1920s. And, as it turned out, this was only the beginning of the story.

Meanwhile, a man on a Sunday morning stroll happened to come on four packages wrapped in newspaper lying in disarray on the road. When he opened one and found a small human arm, he immediately phoned police. Detectives arrived shortly thereafter and discovered that the other packages contained a second arm and each leg. On inspection, they were identified as Marion's severed limbs. Roughly an hour after that discovery, two boys were hiking through the woods and discovered a similar package lying in a gully. It contained the remainder of Marion's body—from the waist to the knees. With these portions of Marion's corpse, Dr. Wagner was able to examine Marion's complete body albeit in fragmented form. Once again, he found no contusions or abrasions. He could not say whether Marion was killed before her body was mutilated. Since he could not find any evidence of chloroform or any other anesthetic, he could only imagine the extent of the child's suffering. It was too much even for the experienced doctor to consider.

The police kept the Parkers under surveillance so that no harm could come to any of the other family members. That afternoon, another letter was found in a fire alarm box near the Parker home. It stated,

> P.M. Parker:
> For all the trouble you have caused, Marjorie Parker will be the next victim. Nothing can stop the Fox and they who try will know the penalty. If you warn anyone of this second success, it will mean you next. Try and get me. I am the Fox. You will never know the rest of my success. You will miss her at 12 o'clock.
> The Fox[2]

The police were concerned and confiscated the letter for analysis in their lab. After an expert with the police department performed a handwriting analysis, it was discovered that the kidnapper did not pen this letter. It was merely a hoax.

From evidence on the towel found in Marion's viscera, police searched the Bellevue Arms apartment building, going through every room and interrogating each of the occupants. The search turned up nothing. Later on that same day, however, the police arrested a suspect in Las Vegas. Lewis D. Wyatt was a twenty-five-year-old doctor's son. The privileged Wyatt always appeared to feel he was above the law and had committed offenses against girls in the past. But this was a bit of a long shot, and California police were not satisfied. They believed Wyatt to be too stocky to fit the description of the killer, who was described as having a slight build. And while he had $20 treasury notes in the same style as was given to the kidnapper, the serial numbers did not match those that Perry Parker had noted when he first drew the money from his account. Although the arrest of the suspect was presumptuously announced in the press, it was soon discovered that Wyatt had an airtight alibi. The search for Marion's killer would have to continue.

By this time, the reward for the killer's capture had reached nearly $100,000. Among those who contributed to the fund included Mayor George Cryer, radio evangelist Aimee Semple McPherson, and Governor Clement Young, as well as several private citizens. The Los Angeles City Council offered $10,000; Los Angeles County donated $5,000. Movie mogul Jack Warner, president of the Warner Bros. studio, read that Marion had been a fan of his company's Rin Tin Tin productions. He contributed to the reward. So did actress Clara Bow, the screen's popular "It Girl," who was so deeply moved on reading that she had been Marion's favorite actress that she sent a personal letter to the Parker family.

While a manhunt remained under way, the people of Los Angeles reacted in horror. Citizens were wary about leaving their homes. Children were kept from school, and attendance fell sharply. Birthday parties and sleepovers were canceled. It was as if ordinary life was suddenly put on pause out of fear. The fear was not completely unfounded, as Marion Parker's killer was still at large.

Chief of Detectives Herbert Cline issued a statement to the press warning citizens not to impulsively lynch suspects who fit the description of the kidnapper. Although clues kept coming in, no positive identification had yet been made as to the killer's identity. The police knew little. They knew where the criminal's car remained stored. They believed it was the same car that had been stolen from a physician in Kansas City, Missouri, on November 7.

The physician, Dr. Herbert L. Mantz, stated that a few days earlier, shortly after he entered his new car and started the motor, a man came out of the darkness and held a pistol to him. The intruder ordered Dr. Mantz to drive a few blocks, then ordered him to stop the car and get out. He allowed the doctor to take his medical bag, stating, "I hope you don't have to walk far." Mantz commented on the thief's coolness, recalling, "He would just as soon shoot me as not."[3] A stakeout proved futile because the kidnapper never returned for the car. It remained in storage Monday morning.

A handwriting expert carefully examined the ransom notes that had been sent to the Parker family. He stated that the notes from Marion to Perry Parker were indeed written by her. On examining the other ransom notes, however, he believed that at least one might have been written by a woman. The police therefore suspected the possibility of more than one criminal being involved in this case.

While conducting an area search, the police arrested and cleared several suspects. One must consider the lack of technological advancements that we take for granted today. Detectives in 1927 had to rely on what would now be considered primitive methods. These methods were successful, as the annals of solved crimes and captured criminals have proven.

The detectives on the Marion Parker case followed every conceivable lead. They didn't want any possibility overlooked. Detective Cline interrogated Earl Smith, who was booked on suspicion of grand larceny, and was acquainted with the Parker twins and their older brother, William. Police still believed the kidnapper had to have some knowledge of the family in order to have pulled this off. His indicating specifics to Mary Holt at Marion's school, well enough to dupe the careful administrator, was proof enough for law enforcement officials that the kidnapper was acquainted with the family. But it was not Earl Smith. He was eventually cleared of having any connection to Marion's kidnapping or murder.

Another arrest involved twenty-two-year-old Lillian Padley, a telephone operator who ran from her apartment during a police search, screaming, "I didn't kill her! I didn't kill the little girl!"[4] Police found what may have been bloodstains in her apartment and flirted with the possibility that she may have been an accomplice. The bloodstains turned out to be wine stains, and her charge was no more than "maudlin drunkenness."

Another man who was being sought as a possible suspect leaped from a train near Saugus, California, as searching officers boarded it. They had been tipped off that a man answering the killer's description had boarded the northbound train at the San Fernando station.

As the suspect jumped from the train, he was followed by bullets from the rifle of a deputy sheriff. The suspect was captured and identified as J. Orville Turley, who had escaped from the Colorado State Prison a few months before. He had been imprisoned for murdering a woman in that state and stuffing her body into a furnace. But he had no connection whatsoever to the Parker case.

On Monday morning, a coroner's inquest was held. Mrs. Mary Holt, the woman at the school who allowed the kidnapper to escort Marion into his car, was among the three people who had been called to testify. Another was Dr. Wagner, who said through tears that the autopsy of his little neighbor friend was the most difficult task of his professional career. The third was a detective, Lieutenant W. W. Warren.

Of the kidnapper, Mrs. Holt stated, "He seemed very well educated and was very courteous and calm. He completely convinced me, and I am always very careful about excusing children, even questioning parents as to identity and reason for the desired absence. I shouldn't have let her go. If I had questioned him in the least . . ." Mrs. Holt dissolved into sobs. She had to be escorted out by her husband. The persnickety schoolmarm who was noted for being so careful chose to let her guard down only once. The results were tragic. [5]

Although the Parkers did not blame Mrs. Holt for Marion's murder, she never forgave herself. The school also supported her. In an effort to offer support to her colleague, Principal Cora Freeman stated she would likely have done the same thing under the same circumstances. Mrs. Holt was eventually too upset to continue working at the school. She remained haunted by her decision for the rest of her life. The coroner's jury returned a verdict of "death at the hands of a person or persons unknown to the jury, acting with homicidal intent."

The Parker family tried to deal with their grief. Perry Parker told the press, "This is the saddest time of my life. Gentlemen, I can't say much. My heart is too full. I know you want some kind of a statement but what can I say? My little girl is gone; gone from me forever. And when I think how . . ." [6]

Parker's eyes filled with tears. He could say no more.

The following morning, Perry W. Parker, Marion's twenty-year-old brother, agreed to speak on his family's behalf. With his father emotionally bankrupt, he assumed the role as man of the family. "Mother knows that Marion is dead, but she doesn't know everything. Father and I know, but, of course, we have not told her how and we never will tell her. Father is asleep at last. He's worn out." [7] Perry Parker had collapsed from exhaustion, not having slept much in the past few days. The stress had been tremendous, but he ventured on until the final, tragic results. His son, also grief stricken at the fate of his beloved little sister, looked after the family, allowing the father a much-needed rest.

On Monday afternoon, the Parkers held a private funeral service for Marion at Forest Lawn Cemetery's Little Church of Flowers in Glendale, California. The chapel was filled with tributes from across the country, but the attendance was limited to Marion's family, selected schoolmates and neighborhood children with whom she closely socialized, and the family's dearest friends. The Reverend Herbert Booth Smith conducted the service. He was the pastor of Immanuel Presbyterian Church, where Marion attended Sunday school.

The Parkers did not want the press descending on their private funeral service and told the police to keep them away. Guards were stationed in front of the Forest Lawn entrances, and reporters were kept from entering the area. Detectives accompanied the Parkers to Marion's funeral service. The funeral was held without incident. Marion's remains were cremated. The gold urn bearing her name still rests in a glass-enclosed crypt at Forest Lawn Cemetery in Glendale.

CHAPTER 6

As the Parkers dealt with their grief and the nation grieved with them, the police were aided by volunteers from the American Legion as well as many private citizens in hunting for the killer of Marion Parker. In all, 7,000 peace officers and 12,000 volunteers were involved in the manhunt. Even those generating the most marginal suspicion were questioned and released only after detectives were absolutely certain that they had nothing to do with Marion's murder. Although the Chrysler coupe had been abandoned, there was one important slipup. The kidnapper failed to wipe the car of fingerprints before leaving it in the parking garage. These fingerprints were instrumental in identifying another suspect.

His name was William Edward Hickman.

Fingerprint expert Howard L. Barlow of the Los Angeles police was the one credited with identifying the prints. They matched up with fingerprints in existing juvenile court records of an old bank forgery case as well as with the fingerprints on the ransom messages sent to Perry Parker. Hickman was only nineteen years old, not between twenty-five and thirty as the description available to the press had initially indicated. As the investigation continued, the information that was acquired indicated that Hickman was a resident of the Bellevue Arms Apartments, which was the apartment complex identified by the towel that had been stuffed into part of Marion Parker's body. The police had already conducted a search of the Bellevue Arms Apartments and had come up with nothing.

Further investigation revealed that William Edward Hickman was registered there under the name of Donald Evans. Other tenants recalled that "Evans" drove a Chrysler coupe like the one attributed to the kidnapper. This "Donald Evans" had reportedly vacated his apartment a couple of days earlier. He left in such a hurry; there were remnants of a half-eaten breakfast still on the table. A thumbprint on the sugar bowl matched up with the other fingerprints, and half a hazelnut was found in the wastebasket. It corresponded exactly with another half of a hazelnut that had been found wrapped in one of the coverings around Marion Parker's torso.

According to his neighbors, the suspect had been in and out of the apartment on Sunday when police were conducting their initial investigation. It was concluded that Hickman, as Evans, was likely out of the building at the time the police were there, which accounted for why he wasn't discovered. Police did not appear to have searched any apartments where nobody was at home. However, now this apartment was being thoroughly investigated.

As detectives continued to carefully search Hickman's apartment, they also found the Gillette razor blades that the kidnapper had threatened (over the phone to Perry Parker) to use on Marion if her father did not comply with his ransom demands. There were bloodstains, copies of newspapers telling of the kidnapping, and a burned memo that appeared to be a rough draft of one of the ransom letters to Perry Parker.

The apartments were located at 11 Bellevue Avenue, which was five minutes from the center of town. From its location, it was easy to access the route on which the kidnapper drove to dump the various packages containing Marion Parker's remains. The juvenile court records indicated that Hickman had forged more than a dozen checks since April 1927. He was employed as a messenger for the Los Angeles First National Bank, the same bank at which Perry Parker was employed as an assistant cashier. The total of Hickman's forgeries was nearly $400.

Police reported that Hickman was discharged from his position at the bank, but while being tried, he asked for and received probation. He attempted to get his former job back but was rejected. It was therefore being assumed by police that Hickman might very likely have held a grudge against Perry Parker, even though Parker had nothing to do with his or anyone's hiring or firing. The police came to the initial conclusion that Hickman's grudge evolved into an obsession and, ulti-mately, that he desired revenge. Rather than go directly after Perry Parker, he chose to harm one of his children. Police recalled other, similar crimes and included in their initial, speculative written reports that this was likely Hickman's modus operandi. [1]

Hickman's mother, Eva, lived in Kansas City with his seventeen-year-old sister Mary in two rooms on the third floor of the residence of Mrs. A. Frank Bash. She had not lived with her husband, Edward's father, for seven years and claimed they were now divorced. It was in Kansas City where Dr. H. L. Mantz had his car, the Chrysler coupe, stolen from him. The evidence against Hickman now became over-whelming. Eva Hickman was stunned that her son, who went by his middle name of Edward, was being formally charged with the kidnap-ping and murder of Marion Parker. She told the Kansas City news-papers, [2] "It can't be so; my boy could not do a thing like that. There is a terrible mistake somewhere. I know my boy could not be guilty of such an unspeakable thing. This was the act of a fiend. My boy is a good clean boy. He could not have done it. I will not believe it until he tells me with his own lips. There is a mistake somewhere."

Mrs. Hickman admitted that her son had gotten into trouble in Los Angeles by forging checks at the bank where Perry Parker was one of the officers. But she also stated that he had since moved back to Kansas City and had been a solid, hardworking citizen. Mrs. Hickman also stated that her son had an interest in drama. He went to California in an attempt to break into the movies. Achieving no success, he took a job at the bank. After being put on probation and losing his job, Hickman returned to Kansas City. It was there that on November 7 he stole Dr. Mantz's car, which hardly describes the work of a "good clean boy." Eventually, Hickman ended up back in California.

Evidence against Hickman continued to pile up. When shown a picture of Edward Hickman, an increasingly more frail, trembling Mrs. Mary Holt, the school official, tearfully identified the man in the photo as the same one whom she allowed to escort Marion Parker from the building on that Thursday.

On being given Hickman's name, Perry Parker remembered the young man all too well. The eerie familiarity of the kidnapper's speaking voice now made sense. Talking to the press, Perry Parker stated, [3] "After the search through employees' records, the photographs, and incidents that have been revealed by the work of the police, I recall the unusual manner in which Hickman talked with me about his discharge for forgery. I remember how he asked for his position again after being granted probation, and his replies to questions, and the calm manner and voice I heard over the telephone, and lastly the coolness and nerve displayed Saturday night when we met for the exchange, and I am convinced that William Edward Hickman was at the other end of the telephone and that he took the $1,500."

Despite his belief that the police were correct in naming William Edward Hickman the killer of his little girl, Parker still did not understand how there could be any motive: "I cannot call to mind any words of madness or revenge that passed while I was talking with Hickman, but I do remember that his reactions to the forgery charges did seem to me to be unusual. He evinced no nervousness and showed very little concern over the seriousness of his actions. This impressed me very much at the time, but no thought of his planning to harm me or members of my family in return for his discharge entered my mind."

The local newspapers in Kansas City where Hickman was living included testimonials from former teachers and friends insisting that he could not possibly have committed such a heinous crime. However, Charles Dowling, a trustee who shared a cell with Hickman the previous June, indicated that Hickman told him he owned some surgical instruments that he kept at home. Dowling further stated that Hickman also had a keen interest in poisons and their various uses and effectiveness.

Hickman appeared to present a classic dichotomy in personality. On the one hand, he seemed adept at offering an outward appearance of confidence, kindness, and a relaxed, comfortable manner. It was enough to cause the persnickety schoolmarm Mary Holt to lower her formidable guard and allow him to take Marion from the school. Thus, to fool a hometown acquaintance into believing that he was a nice boy who could never have perpetrated such a hideous act was probably pretty easy. On the other hand, the other portion of his personality was sinister. From petty crimes to evil thoughts, Hickman had grandiose ideas about kidnapping, poison, surgical tools, and so on but none of the concentration or skill to perpetrate such an act effectively. Something happened from the time he picked up Marion from school and when he

secured the ransom from her father. But it would take the capture of
Hickman to find out.

This would also be necessary to understand what occurred from that
day in early November, when he stole a car in Kansas City, until nearly
a month and a half later, when he kidnapped Marion in California. The
coroner revealed that Marion had been dead only about three hours
when her body was dumped on the street that dark Saturday night. The
people of the nation had similar questions. What had occurred from the
time he escorted her from school on Thursday until the time of her
murder? What was his motive for kidnapping her? Why such a relatively
small ransom demand? Why did he feel it necessary to end her life?
What was done to her before she was killed? And, most shockingly, was
she alive or dead when dismembered?

While the public had its curiosities, everyone realized that the answers may prove to be too gruesome to be detailed in the press. Imaginations ran wild. Hickman was considered a monster of the most heinous order. The public sought vengeance. Newspapers across the country continued to keep their readership up to date on the Marion Parker
case. Now that a suspect had been identified, accompanied by piles of
solid evidence, the search became even more intense. William Edward
Hickman's picture was printed in virtually every newspaper in the United States. Searches were established throughout California; in Kansas
City, where his mother lived; and in Arkansas, where he was born and
spent his childhood, and roadblocks were set up on the Mexican border.
Police did not want Hickman crossing the border to safety and never
revealing the details of his crime or paying for it with his own life.

The Marion Parker murder had become the crime of the century.
William Edward Hickman was a hunted man. Police intensified their
investigation by interrogating virtually anyone who had any contact with
Hickman. The public had questions as well. Not only did they wonder
about the exact circumstances of Marion's murder and dismemberment, but they wanted to know more about her killer. Was this Hickman a career criminal, or was the murder and dismemberment of Marion Parker a random act of unbridled passion? Who was Hickman?
What led him to this terrible crime? Reporters clamored for interviews
with family and old friends. From this, they were able to piece together
the sordid, erratic life of William Edward Hickman.

CHAPTER 7

William Edward Hickman was born on February 1, 1908, in Hartford, Arkansas, to William and Eva Hickman. Because of having the same first name as his father, Hickman was always referred to as either Edward or Ed.

When Hickman was twelve, his parents separated, and his mother moved him, his three older brothers, and his younger sister to Kansas City, Missouri. Hickman was a popular and successful student at Central High School. He was vice president of his senior class, president of three honor societies, editor of the school yearbook, business manager of the school paper, and a member of the debating team and had a seat on the Student Council. He even received an award as the school's best boy orator. Under his 1926 graduation picture, it states that his excellent scholastic standing, unequaled record in extracurricular activities, and high standard of ideals will fix his memory in the annals of Central. According to his mother, Hickman also attended First Baptist Church in Kansas City and played on the Sunday school basketball team.

Hickman's mother, Eva, was more than merely a worrier. Those who knew her described her as very deeply disturbed. While she was pregnant with Edward, her fourth child, she was fraught with a series of emotional disturbances, some of them stemming from her husband's philandering. Physicians have stated that such emotional problems can affect fetal development. Edward was born prematurely and was initially thought to be stillborn, but after some work by doctors, the baby began to breathe. After a few months, Edward was developing in a normal, healthy manner. During Ed's early childhood, Eva Hickman spent most of her time in a fragile emotional state. When pregnant with Ed's sister Mary, two years younger to the day than Edward, Eva would lapse in and out of coherence, even threatening to do harm to her family. Eva would frequently threaten suicide during this time and even attempted to poison herself on at least one occasion. When Edward was three years old, his mother spent a year in the State Lunatic Asylum in Little Rock, Arkansas.

It was during the spring of 1921 when Eva Hickman left her husband and traveled with her children to Kansas City in search of a new life. Edward made friends easily and immediately became active and popular in school. He maintained this status throughout high school, enjoying success in all of his many activities. For those years, Hickman was happy, and his life continued to progress in a positive direction. The success he enjoyed strengthened his self-esteem, and his friendly, relaxed manner attracted a lot of friends. He was popular, outgoing, and good at everything he tried. But his real talent was in debating.

After being awarded for his oratory skills, Edward set out to win a national competition. He worked extremely hard and was very particular about getting his delivery down just right. Edward put a tremendous amount of pressure on himself and spent an entire year preparing for the contest. However, when he lost during the finals and received only a $5 consolation prize, his hopes were completely crushed. Everyone felt that the ordinarily carefree boy would get over it rather quickly, but instead he brooded for a long time. There was a noticeable change in Edward Hickman. And the change was for the worse.

Edward stopped hanging around with his friends. He would not even go to the door when they would come to call. He avoided others at school. Eventually, the friends stopped showing up. Along with his social skills going from gregarious to withdrawn, Edward also redirected his perspective on working toward any goals. After his paltry showing in the national oratory contest following a year of hard work, he felt there was no use working hard toward anything. Rather than act, Edward now spent time pondering. He worked a few jobs here and there, but he couldn't generate any enthusiasm for what he was doing. Hickman had become used to success, at achieving anything he tried. So when he finally attempted something within his area of expertise and came up short, his reaction was far more emotional than those around him would have expected.

Although eventually he had gradually started to become active in clubs once again during his senior year of high school, his interest was always short lived. Edward would join several clubs, exhibit some enthusiasm at first, and then eventually start quitting these activities one by one. By the spring of his senior year, he was more withdrawn than ever. The normally easygoing boy was now often displaying surly behavior, nervousness, and depression. Along with disassociating himself, Edward's grades in school also began to fall. He had always been a very responsible student, but he now exhibited far less enthusiasm, and his academic level soon plummeted.

The only time he seemed to show the caring person he had once been was while visiting his childhood friend Vincent Doran, who lived across the street. Doran was suffering from tuberculosis and would receive visits from a compassionate Edward Hickman almost daily. Hickman would tell jokes, describe films he had seen, lend Doran books, and even play a guitar and sing to him. The Doran family allowed few people to see Vincent, but Edward was always welcome. Vincent had been an avid moviegoer, so he would sometimes read the film ads in the newspaper, longing to attend, and wait for his friend Edward Hickman's vivid description of what happened in the picture. When Vincent Doran died in February 1926, Edward was among the pallbearers at his funeral.

Hickman's attitude suddenly changed when the next annual oratorical contest came up. Edward once again threw himself into the contest in hopes of winning national recognition. The poor showing that had so severely impacted his attitude about everything was such that he wanted to somehow rectify that loss. Practicing heavily with a friend, Rebecca Tomlin, Hickman was adamant that he would avenge the loss he had suffered the year before. He once again was very careful to get everything right. And because of the attention he placed on this contest, his grades continued to be lackluster. It was all for naught. During the finals in April 1926, however, Edward once again received only the $5 consolation prize. He took it even more seriously than the previous attempt, pondering his failure obsessively, wondering aloud if he was good for anything. He never spoke to Rebecca Tomlin again.

People who knew him during this time told journalists that he was a good, kind boy who simply had taken his failures a bit too personally. It was very difficult for them to believe he was capable of something so heinous as the murder and dismemberment of a twelve-year-old girl. Those familiar with Hickman during his boyhood in Arkansas felt generally the same. It seemed virtually impossible that he could be a murderer. But there was another side to Edward Hickman that would be revealed only on further investigation.

After a summer of odd jobs on graduation, Hickman enrolled in Kansas City Junior College. He lasted only nine days, then simply stopped attending. He worked at a few more odd jobs, including the public library, and then at the Kiger Jewelry Company with a recommendation from J. L. Laughlin, the vice principal of Central High School.

While working at the library, Hickman became friendly with a man named Welby Hunt. Edward quit his job at Kiger's, and by late November, he and Hunt committed an armed robbery at a confectionary. They got away with $70. Both Hickman and Hunt were restless. With a car, guns, and some money, they felt they could expand their horizons. It was early December 1926 when they headed for California. Hickman told his mother he was going to again try getting into the movie business.

Like many people during the 1920s, Hickman was quite enthralled with the moving picture. For some, it was (and remains) the ultimate escape from the drudgery of real life. Hickman's oratory skills did not particularly indicate that he had any real talent for acting. And since this was still the era of silent pictures, the ability to deliver dialogue convincingly was not a selling point. But Hickman loved the movies and perhaps was looking for a way to escape into a world that seemed so exciting and romantic on the silver screen. The movies of the late 1920s had perfected the art of comedy, drama, thrills, and suspense. By 1927, the film industry had weathered such scandals as the Roscoe "Fatty" Arbuckle murder trial, the drug addiction of Wallace Reid, and the mysterious death of superstar Rudolph Valentino. The movies seemed to be above the law.

Hickman and Hunt were in Los Angeles on Christmas Eve when they pulled their next robbery. They entered a pharmacy occupied by proprietor Ivy Thoms, his wife, and three customers. Brandishing their pistols and wearing masks, the two robbers were startled by the entrance of Officer D. J. Oliver, who happened to be walking the beat that night and stopped in simply to visit with his friends Mr. and Mrs. Thoms. Oliver started to raise his hands, pretending to surrender, and then pulled out his weapon. A gun battle ensued, with the inexperienced Hickman and Hunt both firing wildly as they ran out of the store. The police officer was hit in the abdomen but survived. Thoms was struck in the chest and killed.

Hickman and Hunt got no money, but they did get away. By the next month, both were working as pages at the First National Trust and Savings Bank, where Perry Parker was employed. Parker's job was such that he likely never really noticed Hickman in his relatively benign role as a page until Edward was finally caught forging checks. After being put on probation for forgery, Hickman returned to Kansas City and spent six weeks during the fall of 1927 as an usher at a movie theater there. The lure of the cinema remained too great, however, and Hickman was fired from the theater for spending too much time sneaking in to watch the movies.

Edward was not in Kansas City for very long when he resumed his criminal activities. In October, he stole a car from a traveling salesman and drove it all the way to Chicago. On October 11, 1927, a man whose description matched Hickman's strangled a young girl in Milwaukee, Wisconsin. When Hickman's picture was published in newspapers throughout the country as the man suspected of killing Marion Parker, the Milwaukee police requested that once Hickman was captured, he be interrogated as to the murder in their city as well.

Hickman went to Michigan, then to Philadelphia. In Chester, Pennsylvania, on October 29, 1927, a gas station manager named James Claire was shot and killed during a robbery by a man whose description matched Hickman's. Just as with the Milwaukee murder, the Pennsylvania authorities recognized Hickman's picture once it was plastered over every newspaper in the nation for the Marion Parker case. They, too, requested he be questioned about the Claire murder.

Along with his crime spree, oddly enough, Hickman also did some sightseeing. He drove into Gettysburg and attended a tour of the Civil War battlefield site. He drove through Maryland and Washington, D.C. He spent a short time in New York, then headed through West Virginia and into Ohio, where he successfully robbed three stores in a mere half-hour time frame. By the time he returned to Kansas City to abandon the stolen vehicle, he had driven in excess of 4,000 miles and had successfully committed several more petty robberies.

It was November 7, 1927, when Edward stole the infamous Chrysler coupe from Dr. Herbert Mantz. Eleven days later, he was back in California, where he robbed a pharmacy of $30. It was then that he settled into an apartment at the Bellevue Arms and pondered his next move.

On Thanksgiving Day, November 23, 1927, Hickman was taking a joyride in San Diego when he met a couple that needed a lift to Los Angeles. Hickman agreed to give them a ride, and the three became friendly. The man and Hickman, in fact, made plans to meet three days later to commit some robberies. They robbed a pharmacy on November 27 and two more pharmacies on December 5. Along with the money, Hickman was asking to be given sleeping tablets and chloroform. When his accomplice asked him why he wanted these items, Hickman explained that he had an idea about committing a bigger crime to net some real money—possibly kidnapping a child for ransom.

CHAPTER 8

William Edward Hickman had achieved a level of infamy in a matter of days. He was now identified as the man who kidnapped, killed, and dismembered twelve-year-old Marion Parker. The country was in a collective state of shock that was presented as anger and disgust. The newspapers continued to give as many details as possible. A man had killed a child, delivered a portion of her body in a sack to her father, and was still at large.

Despite the valiant efforts of many police officers as well as private citizens, the fugitive William Edward Hickman remained elusive. There were literally hundreds of leads, all of which failed quickly. There was at least one report that Hickman was asking directions to Tijuana, Mexico, which would have effectively allowed him to escape the consequences of his crime. A posse from the Los Angeles Police Department remained stationed near the Mexican border.

On the afternoon of December 21, the Los Angeles County chemist announced that there was no trace of chloroform or ether in Marion Parker's lungs. It led Chief of Detectives Herman Cline to the conclusion that she might have been fully awake when dismembered. It was a terribly gruesome thought and one that actually caused the hard-boiled detective to shudder. It also made him even more passionate about capturing the fiend who committed so horrible an act.

Another of Cline's problems was handling a vindictive, bloodthirsty citizenship. Hickman's photo was run in virtually every newspaper in the country. His plain, reasonably attractive, youthful features and dark curly hair were just ordinary enough so that many other men in his general age group had essentially the same features. The result was that many innocent young men were victims of mob violence, and some were actually arrested by police on suspicion.

Michael O'Neil, a twenty-seven-year-old resident of Palms, California, was taken into custody five different times because of his resemblance to Edward Hickman. O'Neil was good-natured about it and told the last officer who nabbed him that he wasn't exactly angry but was becoming frustrated and annoyed by the inconvenience. Detective Herman Cline felt sorry for the young man and wrote a letter that was distributed to police officers not to arrest him again. O'Neil was even given a pass to carry around with him, signed officially by Cline, that indicated he was, in fact, not the killer Edward Hickman. Others were even less fortunate. At least one man was attacked by an angry mob of private citizens who mistook him for Hickman and began beating him in the street. Police came, broke up the fight, proclaimed the man's innocence, and took him into custody. They placed him in a jail cell for his own protection.

Milton Jakowsky was acquainted with members of the Parker family and decided to conduct an investigation of his own in an effort to help the police. Although he was essentially playing the part of a Good Samaritan, in the midst of his investigation, police became suspicious, and he was detained for questioning. Jakowsky was released, but he told the press he would refrain from any further investigating on his own.

A man by the name of Richard Pieaux was arrested in Tucson, Arizona, as a suspect. He showed a card that was supposedly from Cline, but Cline denied any knowledge of giving one to this man. He was held pending further investigation. Along with action in the California area, there were also police stationed in Hickman's recent home of Kansas City, Missouri, and even his birthplace of Hartford, Arkansas, where he spent his early childhood. During the search, there were hundreds of reports from various citizens indicating they had seen a man who fit Hickman's description or who looked like the photo of Hickman that had been printed in the newspapers. The police acted on all of these reports, but none seemed to pan out. Meanwhile, Hickman remained a free man, and nobody knew where he was. In the event that he was arrested or detained on any other charge or even on suspicion by police in another city, police reported Hickman's fingerprint classification in the press: 25 over 1, dash over U, double 0 over double 0, and 14 over 13.

Dr. Herbert Mantz, whose Chrysler coupe had been stolen by Hickman the previous November, was in the news once again. A threat was made to Mantz on December 20 at 3:00 p.m. Detectives, realizing that Mantz could be in danger, happened to be present when a phone call came through, allegedly from Hickman. Picking up a long-distance call at his office, Mantz was startled to hear a familiar voice on the other end: "I'm the fellow who took you for a ride. Do you recognize my voice? I wouldn't be in all this trouble if it were not for you. I'm going to get one of your girls. You know what will happen to her."[1] Mantz, who had a five-year-old daughter and sixteen-month-old twin girls, became terribly worried. Detectives were unable to trace the call but posted twenty-four-hour guards at his home. A similar call was made to the *Kansas City Star* newspaper. Detectives traced the call to a phone booth in the lobby of the National Bank of Commerce in St. Louis. It made note of the threat to Dr. Mantz.

A report was made that Edward Hickman reportedly traded his gray overcoat for five gallons of gasoline at a Santa Monica, California, service station. The overcoat had originally been described as part of the outfit worn by Hickman on the day he abducted Marion Parker from school. Captain C. T. Truschell, a Culver City motorcycle officer who owned the garage, made the discovery.

On December 21, Hickman was reported to be seeking refuge in his former home of Hartford. A report from a Tulsa, Oklahoma, restaurant owner claimed that a man who fit Hickman's description came in to his establishment, ordered a cup of coffee, and left without paying for it.

Meanwhile, Hickman's mother made public her own distress at the situation. Reporting in the press through the words of her friend Lieutenant Colonel Charles "Cap" Edwards, she stated,[2] "To William Edward Hickman: Your mother is prostrated. Brothers and sister desire you to get in touch immediately with your friend Cap Edwards, who, you know, will see that you are justly and fairly treated. Wire, telephone, or write me at my expense at my home, night or day, or at my office." Despite all of these efforts, Hickman's trail remained cold.

Meanwhile, Chief Cline focused his efforts on gathering more evidence. It was discovered that sometime between December 5 and 10, Hickman sent a coat, vest, pants, and an overcoat to be cleaned. The overcoat was described in the same fashion as the light gray one that the kidnapper wore when he took Marion from school the previous Thursday. Cline also stated that Marion's shoes and socks had not been recovered. He speculated that perhaps more clues could be gained from their discovery.

Further investigation of the apartment that had been occupied by Hickman indicated that a napkin was stained with rouge—the same type applied to Marion's cheeks to help give the appearance of life when her dead body was deposited on the street in exchange for the father's ransom money. This led Cline to believe that the girl was taken to the apartment. Cline stated, however, that while Marion may have been taken to the apartment at some point, he was certain the girl had not been killed there. They still needed to capture and get a full confession from the murderer before they would know just exactly what happened from the time Marion was escorted from school on Thursday and when her incomplete body was tossed onto the pavement from a car the following Saturday night.

Cline also considered that Hickman could well have had accomplices. Police had been told that Hickman and another man were seen early Saturday night carrying several packages and a suitcase to a waiting car at the rear of the Bellevue Arms Apartments.

Detective Cline further stated that Detective Lieutenant McCarron and Chief of the District Attorney's Detectives George Contreras would leave by airplane for New Mexico and Arizona to search the principal cities in these states and issue descriptions and pictures of Hickman throughout the area. Cline assured the grieving Parker family that the killer would be soon caught and receive justice.

Meanwhile, Los Angeles School Board Superintendent Susan Dorsey issued a statement to the press in regard to Mary Holt's unfortunate decision:[3] "Mrs. Holt had no authority to excuse any child from school. That is done by our vice principal and then only at the request of the child's parents or guardian. But in this case there appeared to be an emergency when the man rushed in and claimed that there had been an accident and the child's father was calling for her. I talked to Mrs. Holt and am satisfied that I would have acted as she did if I were confronted with the same circumstances. At that time the vice principal, who is the person in authority entitled to excuse a child from class, was busy with the Christmas program and could not be reached in the few minutes that elapsed. The fact that nothing has ever befallen our schoolchildren in the past is evidence in itself that they are safeguarded as is humanly possible." However, much of this statement rings somewhat false. Red flags abounded. This man seemed unaware of Marjorie, and school officials did not wonder why Marjorie was expected to finish out her school day in the wake of a serious accident involving her father and warranting her sister being removed from school. The vice principal was in the building, so why couldn't Miss Holt double-check with her? Why couldn't she verify this man with a quick call to the bank or the Parker home? Obviously, the Los Angeles School Board was simply covering up the fatally bad judgment of one of its administrators. Mary Holt's hair had turned white since the kidnapping took place.

CHAPTER 9

While school officials clamored to justify Mrs. Holt's tragic decision, Herman Cline fully intended to keep his promise to the Parker family. However, he continued to be fraught with false leads. It wasn't for lack of cooperation. By Thursday morning, a week after Marion Parker was taken from her school, law enforcement throughout the United States was on the lookout for Edward Hickman. He was reported as now driving a stolen green Hudson. The car was reported stolen by its owner, Frank R. Peck. Peck identified Hickman as the car thief when presented with pictures.

Two hitchhikers went to the police in Portland, Oregon, stating they were picked up in Lamoines, California, and, when they returned to their apartment in Portland, identified the driver of the car as Edward Hickman based on photos they saw in the newspaper. The hitchhikers told police that the driver kept a loaded .45-caliber automatic pistol either in the side pocket of the machine or in his hand at all times. They said he was not inclined to be talkative or friendly. He seemed determined to reach a goal with all possible haste but was careful not to break any traffic laws. He was very focused and always on the alert. On their arrival in Portland, the driver got out of the car, and the pistol fell to the sidewalk. He picked it up, got in the car, and sped off.

A report came in that a man matching Hickman's description bought gas from an attendant named King in the state of Washington. King recognized Hickman and got in touch with police. Of course, this could easily have been one of many such reports that had been flooding the

police stations throughout this manhunt. But the driver was in a green
Hudson and paid with a $20 gold certificate. It matched up with the
serial numbers of the ransom money Hickman had received from Perry
Parker. When several photographs, including one of Edward Hickman,
were taken to the gas station by Inspector Frank Collins, the attendant
pointed out Hickman as the customer who purchased gas with the $20
bill.

On receiving word that one of the $20 gold certificates that matched
with the ransom money serial numbers had been spent at a nearby
Seattle gas station, Tom Gurdane, chief of police in Pendleton, Oregon,
teamed up with highway patrolman Buck Lieuallen. Old-fashioned lawmen that they were, Gurdane and Lieuallen decided to attempt heading Hickman off at the pass in true western style. They decided to park
on the major highway that would bring Hickman from Washington to
Oregon in the event that he was headed toward their state. It was a bit
of a long shot, but they felt it was worth their time. The two drove to
Echo, Oregon, which is twenty miles outside of Pendleton. Gurdane
had no jurisdiction away from his own city, so it was Lieuallen who was
driving. Since Hickman was described as armed and dangerous, Gurdane had his gun ready to shoot and kill the suspect if necessary.

After a long while, a green Hudson came past, but at first the lawmen figured it would not be Hickman because it had Washington
plates, not California ones. Deciding to make sure, Gurdane and
Lieuallen made a U-turn and went after the vehicle with their siren
blaring. There was no chase. The man in the Hudson pulled over. Two
passengers accompanied him.[1]

"Was I speeding?"

Although the sky was gray and overcast that day, the driver was
wearing sunglasses. He was asked his name.

"My name is Peck."

The driver further stated that he was from Seattle, had been going to
school there, and was traveling to visit family.

He was asked to step out of the car.

As the driver exited the vehicle, a pistol dropped from his lap and
clattered onto the ground. Gurdane drew his weapon and asked about
the gun. The driver indicated that it was for general protection while
traveling. Travelers often carried handguns during the 1920s, especially
in Oregon, which was still cowboy country. Even Gurdane was noted

for frequently wearing full cowboy garb while off duty, the consummate western lawman. Gurdane was also a veteran of law enforcement and quite savvy about the way things were ordinarily. He had a strong suspicion that this errant handgun was more than merely carried for protection. That this familiar character had it was too much of a coincidence. Not succumbing to the man's relaxed charm the way a learned school official had, this rustic lawman decided that further investigation was necessary. The passengers were asked to leave the vehicle.

The lawmen searched the Hudson and noticed a sawed-off shotgun on the floor of the car on the driver's side, sticking out from beneath the seat. They also found another automatic pistol and $65 on the driver's person. Then they found a $1,000 worth of $20 gold certificates in the glove compartment. Lieuallen pulled out the money and showed it to Gurdane.

"You're Hickman," Gurdane accused. "I knew it!"

The exhausted driver put up no defense. "Yes," he said, "I am Edward Hickman."[2]

Hickman was immediately taken into custody, as were his two companions. They protested their innocence, but the two lawmen wanted everything sorted out at the police station. Realizing that they were in no danger, the passengers agreed to assist officers with any information they might know. As was his modus operandi, Hickman appeared surprisingly calm, the same demeanor he seemed to project in any dangerous situation. "I guess it's all over," he said a bit too matter-of-factly.

The passengers in Hickman's car turned out to be another pair of hitchhikers he had picked up in an effort to keep police off his trail. Hickman realized that lawmen were looking for a lone fugitive; he felt the extra people in the car might be enough to throw them off his trail. Bill and Jack Merrill had no idea they were traveling with a hunted man. On hearing that their driver was the notorious Edward Hickman, the two brothers were eager to give any necessary information to police in hopes that it would be helpful. They were detained for rudimentary questioning but only briefly. Bill Merrill later stated that if he and his brother had realized their driver was the hunted Edward Hickman, they likely could have captured him without a bit of trouble. "We had the drop on him."

Hickman was taken into custody and brought to the Pendleton city jail. A crowd gathered as news of his capture spread through the city.

The crowd did not seem vengeful, however. It appeared they were merely curious. The same could not be said for Los Angeles crowds. The night before, a robbery suspect named Ralph McCoy was caught after a chase in downtown Los Angeles. Onlookers yelled that the suspect was "that child murderer William Edward Hickman," even though McCoy looked nothing like the alleged kidnapper and killer of Marion Parker. McCoy was brought to the city jail and placed with other prisoners and was later found strangled in his cell. Each of the other prisoners was questioned. They insisted that McCoy killed himself with his own necktie. Chief Herman Cline asked that extra guards be posted around Hickman.

"Thank God, they've got him," Cline was reported as saying. "I was afraid Hickman would be killed on sight and that we would then never know the details of this horrible tragedy." District Attorney Keyes added, "We know that we have the arch criminal in California murder history. We are devoted to speeding this case to trial."

The Parker home had been guarded all day by three plainclothes lawmen: two inside the house and one outside. Guards were also stationed at the homes of ex–Police Commissioner I. W. Birnbaum and autopsy surgeon Fredrick Wagner, both of whom were considered key witnesses. The Los Angeles Police Department was taking no chances.

A policeman arrived at the Parker house and reported Hickman's capture to the guard stationed outside the home. The guard went inside and quietly told Perry Parker. Parker took his wife Geraldine into another room to give her the news. He also told his son. Geraldine Parker had been under constant treatment by a physician since Marion's murder. Neither she nor Marion's twin sister, Marjorie, were ever told the specific details of the crime.

Perry Parker made a statement to the press:[3] "I am certainly thankful. I am thankful not only for myself, but for the parents of all other children that such a dangerous man has been apprehended. This thing is too terrible to talk about adequate punishment for the man. This strain has been terrible on all of us; I am reassured and only hope there has been no mistake." Parker further stated that he was comfortable allowing the law to take matters into its own hands, believing completely in the American system of justice.

Immediately on word that Hickman had been arrested in Oregon, a Los Angeles County grand jury was convened for a special session at

7:30 p.m. It soon returned an indictment for murder and kidnapping. A warrant was issued, and Hickman was ordered held without bail. Extradition papers were being rushed.

Chief of Detectives George Contreras of the district attorney's office flew to the Oregon area the next morning. Detective Lieutenants H. G. Taylor and E. M. Hamren accompanied Contreras to guard Hickman on his return trip to Los Angeles. Detective Cline stated that extradition papers would be picked up by the officers at Sacramento, where Governor Young promised to have them by the time police arrived. Cline assigned an extra guard to bring Hickman back to protect the accused kidnapper and murderer against being lynched by an angry mob of citizens.

After the indictment, Hickman was told that he had been named the murderer of Marion Parker. His initial, impulsive reaction was to laugh out loud. His sudden burst of laughter startled everyone around. He stopped laughing just as abruptly as he started and then turned serious. He asked if they executed by hanging in California. He then realized that he was not in California but that the crime was committed there. Hickman was asked to pose for a press photograph flanked by the two lawmen who brought him in. He asked if he should "look like a crook" in the photo.

Ever since her murder was reported in the Sunday morning newspapers, the nation wanted to know what exactly had happened to Marion Parker, every bit as much as they wanted her killer captured. Where was Marion Parker from the time of her abduction to the time of her death two days later? Had Hickman acted alone, or were there others? What were the exact circumstances of her murder? What sort of suffering did she have to endure? What could possess a human that he would want to kill and dismember an innocent twelve-year-old child? Now that Hickman was in custody, these questions could finally be answered. This would offer closure to the Parker family and to the public. If Hickman were convicted and found guilty of Marion Parker's murder, he would indeed be executed for his crime.

The public knew more about Hickman's background, but they and law enforcement officials wanted details about the crime. In newspapers across the country, a story was slowly unfolding each day. The public read the accounts with careful attention.

It was the captured Hickman himself who put it best:[4] "This is going to be very interesting before it's all over."

CHAPTER 10

Edward Hickman was in custody, and an indictment had been made. Police from Los Angeles were en route to Oregon to pick him up. He then would await trial. If convicted of kidnapping and murdering Marion Parker, he would be executed by hanging. This was California in the 1920s, and hanging was still the preferred method of execution. While the last public hanging in California was back in 1897, private executions by hanging continued in this state until replaced by the gas chamber in 1937.

While waiting for his Los Angeles escorts, Hickman gave a confession to Parker Branin, city editor of the Pendleton *East Oregonian*, and John Beckwith, a court reporter. The nation was eager to find out the route Hickman took and what exactly had happened to the little girl they had come to know through horrid newspaper reports screaming her name.

Hickman admitted that he had first been in Chicago, but he had no idea about the murder of the Milwaukee girl. With Hickman's denial, the trail to that murder went cold, and despite the efforts of area detectives, the murder of the Milwaukee girl was never solved. Hickman told of renting the apartment at the Bellevue Arms just before Thanksgiving and related how he had gone to San Diego on Thanksgiving Day and picked up a couple, whom he identified as Andrew Cramer and a woman whom he called June Dunning. There was a certain noticeable pride as Hickman told how he was living on what he made doing holdups and felt that if he could get acquainted with an older accomplice, they could work with greater efficiency and less risk. "We just held up drug stores and places like that," Hickman said. "That is the reason I had all these guns. That 30-80 belongs to Andrew."[1]

Hickman further stated that his intention was not to become a crook but simply to gather enough money to attend Park College back in Kansas City. He said that if he managed to round up $1,000, he could return to Kansas City, get a part-time job, and have enough for college tuition. He realized that a life of crime meant eventually getting caught. He intended to steal enough for his plans and return to Kansas City.

According to Hickman, Cramer at one point asked what he thought of committing a kidnapping. Hickman recalled that he wouldn't mind doing it, and it was then that he remembered Perry Parker at the bank.

"I happened to remember that Mr. Parker had a daughter," he said. "I was there in the bank several days, and I noticed especially, I remembered it was his daughter and he would take her downtown and buy her lunch and she was around the bank like she was a big man."[2]

Hickman also stated that Marion Parker was not his first choice as a victim. Initially, he thought of Mr. Hovis, a chief officer at the First National Bank, who had a very young child.

"I was afraid it would be harder to handle her," he said. "She was a baby and would probably cry. I thought either Mr. Hovis or Mr. Parker would have sense enough to consider $1,500 an easy settlement in consideration for their own daughter. I meant no harm to either one, but I thought it would be easier to handle the older girl than a little child."

Hickman recalled that he and Cramer went to the Parker home after Hickman found the address in a telephone book. They saw Marion riding her bicycle after she had come home from school.

On Thursday morning, Hickman parked by the house early and watched Marion and Marjorie Parker leave for school. He admitted trying to get their attention as they rode the streetcar, just as Marjorie had told police. It was then that Hickman decided to pick Marion up at school. "There was no plan," he said.

"You have read in the papers how it all happened. I went and told the teacher that her father had been in an accident, and this other girl came over to see which one of the girls I wanted, and I said I wanted the younger one. She looked younger, but it turned out they were twins, but she did not question me in any way. They asked what was her first name, so I told them I didn't think I remembered, but I told them I worked at the bank. I didn't give my real name—I forgot the name I did give them—and they asked me which girl I wanted, and I said the younger one, and she said, 'Marion?' and I said 'Yes, that is the one the father is calling for.'"[3]

It was from this point until her murder that nobody knew what had happened to Marion Parker. As the reporters and guards listened carefully, Hickman related the events that occurred after he escorted the child to his car. Unlike her principal, Marion Parker was immediately inquisitive. "She started asking questions about what had happened and how it happened and who hit him," Hickman said, "and I answered all of her questions."

Marion did not appear to be worried that she was in any danger but did express great concern about her father's well-being. As they drove on, Hickman and Marion had a general conversation about the movies and other similar interests. Hickman related how his favorite actress was Esther Ralston. Marion talked about her favorites like Harold Lloyd, Clara Bow, Douglas Fairbanks, and the canine adventures of Strongheart or Rin Tin Tin that were very popular with children of this era. "I really kind of liked her," Hickman continued. "I could not look her in the face when I told her she was kidnapped. When I told her nothing had happened to her father, she didn't worry or scream or anything. She took it as calm as could be."

They drove around all afternoon, Hickman making stops to send telegrams to the Parker household where the family was waiting nervously. That evening, they went to see the film *Figures Don't Lie* with Hickman's favorite actress, Esther Ralston, at the Rialto Theater in Alhambra, California.

Hickman recalled that the two of them had a good time at the movies. He recalled that Marion liked the movie very much, although this drawing room drama was hardly comparable to the comedies and thrill movies that Marion usually enjoyed. Hickman also indicated that he and Marion laughed a lot at the preceding vaudeville show that opened for the movie. From the way Hickman described it, Marion had a rather pleasant time until factors entered that were out of Hickman's hands.

It was after his and Marion's movie excursion, according to Hickman's confession, that Andrew Cramer got involved. Hickman explained that Andrew Cramer took custody of Marion while Hickman made phone calls and sent the telegrams. He did not see Marion again until Friday night and had her write a letter to her father that made it sound as if she were being treated poorly. Hickman stated that Marion did not seem to like Cramer and would beg to stay with Edward instead. But Hickman claimed that he was intimidated by Cramer and, as a result, made no trouble.

Hickman then claimed that Cramer arrived at Edward's apartment on Saturday and he was holding a suitcase. He opened it up to reveal Marion's decapitated body to a shocked Hickman. Cramer stated that the girl was crying too much, and he decided to stop her permanently. Cramer also indicated that the police were becoming more and more suspicious and that killing Marion would destroy any evidence. As he continued to confess, Hickman stated, "I am terribly sorry she was killed, because I sure liked her." Then Hickman started crying.

Along with naming a guilty accomplice, another surprising thing that Hickman revealed was that when detectives first made a search of the Bellevue Arms, he was at home and actually spoke to them. "The detectives came in and looked around and did not express any suspicion to me at all. I went out in the hallway and talked to seven or eight of the detectives. I asked them if there was anything I could do. They said there wasn't. They searched my apartment and left."

Hickman's confession was stunning and was printed verbatim in many of the major newspapers throughout the country. Smaller papers printed excerpts, some with commentary from editors. Travel was much slower in 1927–1928 than it is in the twenty-first century, so the Los Angeles police were still en route. When word got back to them about Hickman's naming of an alleged accomplice, they were not surprised. They had suspected another man (and a possible woman) as perhaps having assisted Hickman in some manner.

In their subsequent investigation based on Hickman's most recent confession, the Los Angeles Police Department discovered there was not one but two Andrew Cramers. First, there was an Oliver Andrew Cramer, who, like Hickman, went by his middle name. Cramer admitted knowing Edward Hickman. But he had been arrested the previous August and had been incarcerated ever since. He was, therefore, behind bars at the time of Marion's murder. He did, however, state that his brother, whose middle name was also Andrew, had a girlfriend named Dunning and believed that June Dunning may have been that woman's sister.

Frank Andrew Cramer actually did have a girlfriend named Dunning. Her first name was Rose, not June. She did have a sister, but her name was Mabel, and she had died nine months ago. Furthermore, Frank Andrew Cramer was arrested on a different charge right around the time of his brother's arrest. He, too, had been behind bars since August. Furthermore, he was not ordinarily addressed by his middle name as his brother was. Hickman was visibly shaken on being told of Cramer's alibi. But he continued to stick to his story.

Chief Herman Cline had initially believed that Hickman may likely have had help when perpetrating his crime but was having misgivings. About the time of the confession naming Andrew Cramer, Cline had already begun to conclude that Hickman acted alone. "The story of Hickman having an accomplice is an absurdity. We previously have checked out every angle of his asserted accomplice and have found the story false and weak. We are after the truth of this matter, and I am convinced we shall find it when Hickman is faced with the facts by those who know the intricate details of the Parker crime."[4]

For his part, Hickman decided to write a letter for publication in the nation's newspapers, warning other young people about a life of crime.[5] It read,

This affair has gained nationwide publicity and the great reward and search by the police of the west coast show opposition of the American people to criminal tendencies. Kidnappings and savage murders are the worst of America's crimes and everything should be done to prevent anyone interfering in any way with the liberty and life of American citizens. Young men and college students should consider the Parker case as atypical crime of the worst that can happen when a young man gradually loses interest in family, friends, and his own honesty. The young men of this country can see that I can pass as an ordinary young man as far as outward appearances go. Crime in its simplest definition is to have without work and enjoy the same place in society as other people and still show no honest effort or intention to go right. Young men, when crime has once overcome your will power to be honest and straight, you are a menace to society. Take my example to illustrate this. See how I tried to get what every young man wants, but in becoming a criminal to do so I put my

own life in a mess and the way out is dark. Hope I can do some good
by giving you this warning. Think it over, see my mistake. Be honest
and upright. Respect the law. If you do these things you will be
happier in the end and you will have gained much more from your
life.
W. Edward Hickman

Hickman's plea hardly allowed anyone to forget the kidnapping, murder, and decapitation of a twelve-year-old child. But there indeed was a
marginal portion of the population who looked on Hickman as a sort of
martyred celebrity.

Further investigating Hickman's confession and his naming Andrew
Cramer as his accomplice (and the real killer of Marion Parker), Milton
Carlson, a handwriting expert and criminologist, suggested that possibly
Hickman read of the White Chapel murders in London in the 1880s.
Several women were murdered and mutilated, and the suspected mur-
derer, a young student of surgery, although never caught, was found
dead in the River Thames. His name was Andrew Kramer, spelling his
name with a "K" rather than a "C."

The criminologist declared it a trait of the criminal mind to use an
incident or a name out of a case or report of which he had read a great
deal. Hickman, it was assumed, could very well have deluded himself
into believing that he had an accomplice, even if such a person didn't
exist. His changing the first letter of the last name from a "K" to a "C"
was evidently his way of copyrighting the idea for his own use.

But in the end, Hickman knew better, and he realized that he had to
come up with another idea. If his imaginary accomplice could not vindicate him, then perhaps he could somehow manipulate the system. Realizing that his attempt to pin the murder on Andrew Cramer had failed,
Hickman recalled the Leopold and Loeb case, in which the plea was
guilty by reason of insanity. Rather than face execution, Leopold and
Loeb were confined to a mental institution for the remainder of their
lives.

"I wonder if I could pretend I was crazy," he would say to one of the
guards.

"How does a fellow act when he's crazy? Do you just have to talk a
little off, or do you have to rave around?"[6]

Dr. W. D. McCary of Pendleton, who managed more than 1,000
inmates at a nearby asylum, had already examined Hickman.

"His mind seemed clear," the doctor told the newspapers.

"He told a straight, coherent story and never was at a loss for words. There was nothing about him to indicate insanity. He did not differ a bit from hundreds of thousands of other young men.[7]

"As to whether Hickman is given to sadistic practices I cannot tell. I observed him only casually and did not have the opportunity to make a deep study of him. I saw nothing out of the ordinary about him, nothing that would justify a defense of insanity.

"He says that he does not like girls, that he is deeply religious, and that his ambition was to become a minister. Several times he made mention of God, and in discussing his capture took the attitude that since God willed it, it had to be."

But Hickman was making plans, ready to resume the role of his character, the "Fox," for the Los Angeles police, who were soon to arrive. He spent a restless night being taunted by other prisoners, whose angry catcalls were intimidating. And representatives from the Los Angeles Police Department were to arrive by morning and return him to the city of his crime.

Meanwhile, the Parker family had no real plans for the coming Christmas season. The happy spirit that always surrounded this holiday in previous years just wasn't there. Marion's murder was a black cloud that enveloped the Parkers with a greater sorrow than they could ever have imagined. Marjorie would be able to open her gifts, but it would be bittersweet since she and Marion had always enjoyed opening their presents together.[8]

"We have no plans for Christmas," Perry Parker told the press. "But we are trying to bear up under the tragedy as bravely as possible."

CHAPTER 11

Edward Hickman couldn't sleep. The other prisoners were still taunting him. He was genuinely worried about facing the gallows. He was hoping to receive a life sentence instead of being executed.

Hickman planned to present an insanity defense in order to be spared from the hangman's noose, shrewdly concocting a plan the same way he had tried to create and execute the crime that placed him in this situation. He had little quality time to think about it, though, as the catcalls from other prisoners distracted and stressed him out.

While his fellow prisoners were indeed incarcerated for their own crimes, most of them quite ugly in and of themselves, they still banded together and considered Hickman an even greater level of criminal. The act of murdering and dismembering an innocent twelve-year-old girl for the paltry sum of $1,500 was considered to be well beyond the parameters of even the worst crimes committed by the other prisoners. Hickman was a monster to the general public, and this characterization extended well into the sordid world that dwelled behind bars.

By 4:00 p.m. on Saturday, Christmas Eve, Hickman was depleted of energy. He fell onto his cot and slept soundly—so soundly, in fact, that he remained completely still with only the faintest indication of breath. The prison guards would periodically check on him to see if he was still breathing. Hickman was still sound asleep an hour later when representatives from the Los Angeles Police Department arrived to take him back to California.

While the Los Angeles police waited, a Pendleton, Oregon, officer unlocked Edward Hickman's cell and found him asleep on the lower bunk. Hickman was awakened and brought outside of his cell to face the Los Angeles lawmen. Suddenly, Hickman went into hysterics. His body jerked and flailed about as he began screaming Marion's name. He suddenly threw himself onto the floor and began kicking his feet, continuing to scream the murdered child's name. Hickman was restrained and returned to his cell. The Los Angeles police decided to come back later when he was in a more settled state.

During the night, Hickman made two rather foolish attempts at suicide. He began with a headfirst dive from his top bunk onto the floor. For that, he got a headache and a lump on his head but nothing more. Next, he borrowed a handkerchief and tied one end around his neck and the other to the bars. He fell to the floor with his full weight and was choking when a guard came in and cut him down.

It was difficult to determine if these were actual attempts at suicide or part of Hickman's plan to elude the hangman's noose by presenting himself as insane. Some felt these acts were simply part of a series of events designed to build more evidence that pointed to his insanity. The events were documented and did make the papers, and thus, if Hickman was indeed trying to call attention to behavior that could help an insanity defense, his actions were successful. There was a certain perverse irony to Hickman attempting suicide by strangulation in order to avoid being hanged.

The Los Angeles police returned on Christmas morning. Chief of Detectives Herman Cline addressed Hickman directly, indicating that they were going to take him back to Los Angeles. Acknowledging the publicity the case had been getting in all forms of existing media, Cline told Hickman about the movie cameramen that were going to take his picture for their newsreels. Cline pointed out to Hickman that it was up to him as to how he would be presented in these photos and films. Hickman could walk out like a man, or he could once again break down and be seen on camera acting in that manner. It must have been a bit of a conundrum for Hickman. He could use the publicity to appear insane in newsreels across the country. But he decided to instead go out like a man. Still plotting, still calculating, he appeared cool and collected as he left the Pendleton jail for the bus that would take him to the train station. Hickman was handcuffed to his two guards. His left hand was cuffed to Dick Lucas and his right to Harry Raymond. Nobody could shoot Hickman down without also getting both officers. He was safe from the crowd.

On arriving at the train station, Hickman looked at the 500 spectators who showed up to watch him leave the bus and board the train. The sea of angry, vindictive faces shouting threats was representative of how most people felt toward him. Hickman realized this as he studied the vigilant crowd, who would like to have ripped him to pieces if not for the fact that he was heavily guarded by law enforcement. The police realized that some of the onlookers were likely armed.

During the six-hour train ride, Cline bombarded Hickman with questions. Hickman broke down, admitting that it was he who murdered and dismembered Marion Parker. There was nobody named Andrew Cramer. He had no accomplices at all. He had acted alone. Hickman spent four hours relating the story in detail to Cline. He further stated that he planned to plead guilty and use an insanity defense. He therefore wanted the judge to be fully aware of every detail of the story. Hickman agreed to write a full and complete statement. He spent much of the train ride relating just what he would include in the statement. Cline told Hickman that they were interested in a judge being given full details. He encouraged Hickman to tell everything clearly and to include every detail.

Meanwhile, back in Los Angeles, detectives continued their search of Hickman's apartment at the Bellevue Arms and discovered enough clues to indicate that Marion was indeed killed there despite what Cline had believed earlier. And back in Oregon, Tom Gurdane and Buck Lieuallen basked in the spotlight for having captured Hickman. When it came to the reward money, however, they tried to be diplomatic. They stated that they did not want the money of individuals. But they saw no reason why they should not take what was offered by the Los Angeles banks and some of the organizations. That, they believed, was legitimate reward money, legitimately earned.

While Gurdane and Lieuallen seemed the obvious choices for the reward, there were several who claimed a piece of the nearly $100,000 on Hickman's capture, even those with the most marginal contact. Los Angeles Mayor George Cryer appointed a committee of thirteen civic leaders to discuss how the reward money should be distributed.

The train arrived in Portland at 6:10 p.m. but without Hickman. The officers, realizing there would be a crowd, stopped about five miles east at Montavilla, where Hickman was brought to the Portland jail by police car. The 2,000 people who showed up at the Portland station did not see the infamous kidnapper.

After a four-hour wait, Hickman boarded a train headed for Los Angeles. It was then that he began his written statement with the intention of offering every graphic detail about his crime.

CHAPTER 12

Hickman was on board the Union Pacific's Cascade Limited, heading toward California, when he wrote his statement about the Marion Parker kidnapping and murder. This time he would not pepper his story with imaginary accomplices. That ruse had failed.

Perhaps it was the sudden notoriety, the cameras, the newsreel cinematographers, and the massive attention, but Hickman appeared to react differently. He suddenly wanted to tell of the kidnapping and murder. The big crime he wanted to commit had been committed. He had, in fact, committed an act that was considered by the general public as the most heinous crime. Hickman's way with words extended to writing. While his oratory skills surpassed his writing ability, he was still quite capable of presenting his ideas through the written word. He claimed he would now tell everything, including all of the graphic details and his motives. Detective Herman Cline arranged for Hickman to get enough paper. Hickman began to write:[1]

"My name is William Edward Hickman. I was born February 1, 1908 at West Hartford, Arkansas. I desire to make the following statement relative to the kidnapping of Marion Parker in Los Angeles, Thursday, December 15, 1927.

"During the past six months the idea of kidnapping a young person and holding it for ransom came to me as a means of securing money for college. I had already been in touch with President Hawley of Park College near Kansas City, Mo., and was to see him again in February following to arrange my entrance.

"On November 23, 1927, I rented an apartment at the Bellevue Arms house under an assumed name of Donald Evans. At this date I had no definite plans to kidnap, but on Monday, December 12, I decided to locate Mr. Harry Hovis, Chief Teller at the First National Bank of L.A. and arrange to take his young child, but I wasn't satisfied with the situation. I then thought of Mr. P.M. Parker because I had seen a young girl with him one day at the bank while I was employed there as a page. This was the First National Bank at 7th and Spring Sts., and since I thought that the girl with Mr. Parker was his own child, I decided to start with my plans.

"On Wednesday, Dec. 14, I drove out to Mr. Parker's house at 1631 South Wilton Pl. and waited to see him drive home and his daughter return from school. On Thursday Dec. 15, 7:30am, I was again parked near the Parker residence in my car, which I had stolen in Kansas City, Mo., in early November. It had a California license plate, No. 1677679, which I took from a Chevrolet car in San Diego Sunday night, about the 5th of December. About eight o'clock I saw two young girls leave the Parker home and followed them to the Mt. Vernon Jr. High School in that district. I returned to this school later from my apartment at the Bellevue Arms. I entered the attendance office at approximately 12:30 and asked for Mr. Parker's daughter, saying that her father had been in an accident and wished to see her. I gave my name as Cooper and assured the teacher that I was a friend of Mr. Parker's and worked at the First National Bank. I was asked if the girl's name was Marion Parker since it occurred that Mr. Parker had two daughters at the school. I replied in the affirmative and emphasized that it was the younger daughter for whom the father was calling. There was only a slight wait and Marion was called from her class. I told her to come with me, repeating what I had said to the teacher.

"The young girl did not hesitate to come with me and we left the school immediately. I drove east on Venice Blvd. to Western Ave., north on Western to Beverly Blvd., east on Beverly Blvd. to Temple St., on Temple to Glendale Blvd., out Glendale Blvd. through the city of Glendale.

"I stopped the car on a quiet street out in this vicinity and told Marion that she had been deceived. I told her that I would have to hold her for a day or two, and that her father would have to give me $1500. Marion did not cry out or even attempt to fight. She pleaded with me not to blindfold or tie her and promised not to move or say anything. I believed her and took off the blindfold and bandages from her arms and ankles. I warned her that she would be hurt if she tried to get away and showed her my .380 automatic revolver. Marion said she understood and that she didn't want to be shot. I started the car and we drove back to Los Angeles to the main post office where I mailed a special delivery letter to Marion's father. Marion sat right up in the seat beside me and talked in a friendly manner. It was very nice to hear her and I could see that she believed and trusted me for her safety. When I left the post office I drove out to Pasadena. Here I stopped at the Western Union office on Raynold Ave., and left Marion perfectly free in the car while I sent a telegram to her father. I wanted to warn Mr. Parker not to do anything until he got my letter and told him that his daughter was safe. Marion and I left Pasadena and drove out Foothill Blvd. beyond Azusa. We talked and had a jolly time. Marion said she liked to go driving and she went so far as to relate to me that she had a dream just a few days before that someone called for her at the school and in reality kidnapped her. Before dark came I turned back and we stopped in Alhambra where I mailed a second telegram.

"At seven o'clock we went to the Rialto Theater in South Pasadena and saw the picture entitled, *Figures Don't Lie* with Esther Ralston. Marion enjoyed the picture and we both laughed very much during the vaudeville. We left the theater about ten p.m. and drove directly to the Bellevue Arms Apts. Marion, I could see, was a little worried and also sleepy. We sat in the car by the side of the apartment for about thirty minutes and saw a chance to enter without being seen. I told Marion that my room was on the third floor and cautioned her to follow just a few steps behind me. No one saw us go to my apt (No. 315) and when we were inside Marion went to sleep immediately. She chose to sleep on the couch and only took off her shoes and used a heavy blanket, which I gave her for cover. I placed a reading lamp by the door and left it lit so that it cast a dim light over the room. I slept in the bed and retired shortly after Marion. I stayed awake for some time to see that the girl would not attempt to leave the apartment.

"Next morning Marion was awake by seven o'clock. She was sobbing and didn't say much. I got up and prepared breakfast but she said she wasn't hungry. After a while I began to talk to Marion and tried to console her. I told her she could write a letter to her father and that I would also. So she then stopped sobbing and wrote a note and didn't cry any more that day (Friday). About 9:30am I left the apt for about thirty minutes. I went downtown where I got the newspapers and mailed the special delivery letter which included Marion's note. I tied Marion to a chair while I was gone, but used cloth bandages and she was not cut or bruised in any way. I did not blindfold or gag her and she promised to keep quiet. When Marion saw her pictures and name in all the papers she felt sorry, because she didn't want her father to give out the news of her kidnapping because I had told her of all my plans. Later however she seemed to like to look at her picture and kept reading the account of her abduction. Marion didn't want to stay in the apt all day so I promised to take her driving again.

"We left the apt about noon and drove out through Alhambra and San Gabriel, past the Mission Playhouse to San Gabriel Blvd., and turned on the highway toward San Diego near Whittier. We drove through Santa Ana and while we were stopped there for gasoline at a Richfield station I noticed that the attendant looked at Marion very closely. We drove on beyond San Juan Capistrano and stopped to rest the car a while before we turned back. We were about 70 miles out of Los Angeles and it became dark before we got back to the city. I secured some evening papers and Marion read to me as I drove.

"About 7 o'clock I stopped the car just south of 7th Street on Los Angeles St. and left Marion in the car while I went to the Pacific Electric Station at 6th and Main St. and called her father over the telephone. I called twice but the line was busy each time. I told Marion so, and we then drove up Los Angeles St. to Sunset Blvd., and out Sunset to a drug store near Angeles Temple. I called Marion's father and talked to him. He said he had the money and wanted me to bring his girl back to him. He said he'd meet me anywhere and I said I'd call him back. I called the second time from a drug store at Pico and Wilton Sts. at about 8:30 which was 30 minutes later than the first. I told Mr. Parker to get in his car alone and drive north on Wilton to 10th and turn to the right one short block to Gramercy and park on Gramercy, just north of 10th. Marion and I were parked on Pico between Wiltoyn and Gramercy and we both saw Mr. Parker drive by. There were two other cars following his and I feared that some detectives were planning to trap me so Marion and I drove directly back to my apt and didn't go by her father. We got back inside without anyone seeing us. Marion

sobbed a little because she couldn't go home that night but saw everything and was content to wait till the next morning. Marion slept the
same way Friday night as Thursday and we both were awake and up by
7:30am the next morning (Saturday).

"I told Marion to write her father that he must not try to trap me or
something might happen to her. She wrote the note in her own words
and very willingly, the same as in the first note, since she knew my plans
as well as I did and read all of my letters. I told Marion all along that I
would have to make things look worse to her father than they were so
that he would be eager to settle right away. Marion knew that I wrote
her father that I would kill her if he didn't pay me but she knew that I
didn't mean it and was not worried or excited about it. In fact, I promised that even though her father didn't pay me the money, I would let
her go back unharmed. She felt perfectly safe and the tragedy was so
sudden and unexpected that I'm sure she never actually suffered
through the whole affair, except for a little sobbing which she couldn't
keep back for her father and mother.

"I wrote my third letter to Mr. Parker and put it with Marion's note
in the same envelope. I told Marion that I would go downtown again
and get the newspapers and mail the special delivery letter. I said I
would return in less than a half hour and then we would get in the car
and meet her father somewhere that morning. I went ahead and tied
her to the chair as I did Friday morning, except that I blindfolded her
this time, and made ready to leave the apt. She said to hurry and come
back.

"At this moment my intention to murder completely gripped me. I
went to the kitchen and got out the rolling pin, meaning to knock her
unconscious. I hesitated for a second and changed my mind. Instead I
took a dishtowel and came back to where she was sitting on the chair,
pushed back in the small nook in the dressing room, with her back
turned to me. I gently placed the towel about her neck and explained
that it might rest her head, but before she had a time to doubt or even
say anything I suddenly pulled the towel about her throat and applied
all of my strength to the move. She made no audible noise except for
the struggle and heaving of her body during the period of strangulation,
which continued for about two minutes.

"When Marion had passed to unconsciousness and her body stopped
its violent struggle I untied the bandages and laid her on the floor. I

took off her stockings, her sweater, and dress, and placed her in the bathtub. I got a big pocketknife, which I had in the apt and started cutting. First, I cut a place in her throat to drain blood but this was not sufficient. I then cut her arms in two at the elbows and washed and wrapped them in newspaper. I drained the blood from the tub as I cut each part so that no stain was allowed to harden. Next I cut her legs in two at the knees. I let the blood drain from them and washed and wrapped them in newspaper also. I put the limbs in the cabinet in the kitchen and then took the remaining undergarments from the body and cut through the body at the waist. As I cut the limbs and body there were heavy issues of blood and jerks of the flesh to indicate that life had not completely left the body.

"I drained the blood from the midsection and washed and wrapped this part in newspapers and placed it on a shelf in the dressing room. I washed the blood from the tub and separated some of the internal organs from the body and wrapped them in paper. Then I tied a towel about the neck and tied another towel to it and left the upper part of the body to hang until the blood had completely drained from it. I placed a towel up in the body to absorb any blood or anything which I had not dried. I took this part of the body and after I had washed and dried it, wrapped the exposed ends of the arms and waist with papers and tied them so that the paper would not slip. I dressed the body and placed it in a brown suitcase. I combed back the hair, powdered the face and laid a cloth over the face when I closed the suitcase. I put the suitcase on a shelf in the dressing room and then cleaned up the bath trying not to have any traces of blood anywhere.

"I went to the writing desk and wrote a second part to my third letter which I called the final chance terms. I opened the envelope which I had sealed and put this third part with Marion's second note and my third letter. I went downtown and mailed this letter special delivery to Mr. Parker about one o'clock. I then went to the Loew's State Theater, but I was unable to keep my mind on the picture and wept during the performance.

"I returned to my apartment about 5:30 p.m. and took all the parts of Marion's body downstairs to the car waiting by the side entrance. No one saw me and I hurried out Sunset Blvd. and turned to the right at Elysian Park where within 100 yards along the road I left all of these parts.

"I was back at the apt by 6 o'clock and took the suitcase with the upper section and drove to Sixth St. and Western Ave. Here I called Mr. Parker and told him to come to Manhattan Place and park just north of 5th St. I drove around in that neighborhood to see that no police cars were coming before I met Mr. Parker and I stopped between Sixth and Fifth Sts. on Manhattan Place and took the body from the suitcase. I left the suitcase outside the car and before I got back inside I turned one number back from each end of the rear license plate. About eight o'clock I saw Mr. Parker's car where I had told him and as I approached I tied a white handkerchief about my face. I drove up to the side of his car and stopped. I had a shotgun (sawed off) in one hand and I raised it up so that Mr. Parker would see it and cautioned him to be careful. He asked for his daughter and I raised up the head of the child so that he could see its face. He asked if it was alive. I said, 'Yes, she is sleeping.' I asked for the money and he handed it right over to me. I said I'd pull up ahead of him about 50 feet and let the child out. I pulled up ahead and stopped but only leaned over and placed the body on the edge of the fender so that it rolled over onto the street, and then I speeded east on 4th street and downtown where I parked the car at 9th and Grand.

"Note: the knife that I used in the cutting of the child was purchased at a hardware store on South Main Street about 5th Street. I identified this knife to Chief of Detectives Cline who now has it in his possession. He got this knife from my suitcase where I said it was.

"I then went to the Leighton Cafe in the Arcade on broadway, between 5th and 6th sts. I passed one of my twenty dollar gold certificates when I paid for my meal.

"I went back to the apt after I left the cafeteria and retired. On Sunday morning detectives from the police dept. searched my apt for towels but made no arrest. I took my guns and the ransom money and checked them at the P.E. Station near 6th and Main. I also checked a black handbag and a suit box at the station. I went to the Tower Theater early in the afternoon. Shortly after five p.m. I rode out on Hollywood Blvd. on a P.E. car and got off at Western Ave. I entered a closed car parked on Hollywood Blvd. near Western and told the man sitting at the wheel to start the car. He saw my gun and obeyed. We drove several blocks away and I told him to leave the car. Before he did I took about $15 from him. This occurred about six o'clock Sunday evening, and shortly after seven I had secured my packages and grip from the P.E. Station and was on my way out of Los Angeles on Ventura Blvd. I drove overnight and arrived at San Francisco Monday about one p.m. I stopped at the Herald Hotel (room No. 402), and Tuesday about 9:30am I started for Seattle, Washington. I arrived there between 6 and 7 p.m. Wednesday and left about 9:30 p.m. to go back to Portland. I passed two of the gold certificates in Seattle and another on the road about twenty miles south of Seattle. The two bills in Seattle were in the downtown district, one at a clothing store where I purchased a pair of gloves, and a suit of underwear, the other was at a theater.

"Note: While at the Herald Hotel in San Francisco room 402 I assumed the name of Edward J. King, of Seattle. I arrived in Portland early Thursday morning and started on the Columbia River Highway east. Before leaving Portland I left my California license plates and put on two Washington plates which I took from a Ford car in Olympia. On the Columbia River Highway near The Dalles I picked up two boy pedestrians and drove on till within a few miles of the town of Pendelton, Oregon, where I was arrested and taken to the city jail at Pendelton. The statement that I made after arrest implicating Andrew Cramer and June Dunning was false. This is my true statement.

"Note: On the highway north of San Francisco I picked up a man and left him at Redding. I picked up two fellows south of Dunsmuir who rode with me to Portland, Oregon. I might say that the names Andrew Cramer and June Dunning are merely fictitious as far as I know.

"Note: In reference to Marion's body just before I delivered the portion to her father, I used a large needle which I had in my possession and some black thread to fix and hold the upper lids of her eyes open so that her father would think that she was alive when he saw the face.

"This statement is true and made freely and voluntarily by me."

Hickman signed the confession, which was also signed by the lawmen and Hickman's guards, Chief Davis, Dwight Longuevan, Harry Raymond, Dick Lucas, George Home, and District Attorney Asa Keyes. Shortly thereafter, Hickman insisted that he needed to tell more. Apparently, this first confession did not include details that Hickman suddenly felt were important to relate. Asking for more paper, Hickman proceeded to write a second statement, giving his motives for the killing of Marion Parker.

CHAPTER 13

With his second statement, Hickman wanted to offer further clarification of his crime. It appeared he wanted to tell all, perhaps in hopes that the judge and jury would somehow understand his motivation. It has been stated that murderers such as Hickman will frequently have a skewed perspective as to their crimes and the reasons behind these heinous acts. In Hickman's case, he wanted to simply clarify his perspective. Thus, he wrote an accompanying statement:[1]

"My name is William Edward Hickman and this statement was made and witnessed on the S.P. Train en route to Los Angeles. This statement regards the kidnapping and murder of Marion Parker. The time of the murder was Saturday morning December 17, 1927. The place was in room 315 of the Bellevue Arms Apts. in Los Angeles. I wish to explain in full the motives which prompted me to commit this crime.

"In the first place let me say that the only circumstances connecting my intentions of murder to Marion Parker are purely incidental. I was not prompted by revenge in the killing of Marion Parker. Only through my association with Mr. P.M. Parker at the First National Bank while I worked there as a page from January to June, 1927, made it possible for me to see Marion Parker and to know she was P.M. Parker's daughter. This was incidental and I merely picked it up and followed it through. My motives in the murder of Marion Parker are as follows:

"1). Fear of detection by the police and the belief that to kill and dissect the body I would be able to evade suspicion and arrest. I had warned Mr. P.M. Parker to keep the case secret and private but he was not reasonably able to do so. The great publicity and search which followed caused me to use what I considered the greatest precaution in protecting myself. After successfully dodging the authorities for two days I was overcome by such fear that I did not hesitate even to murder to escape notice. I consider that this fear and precaution were the result of my instinct for self-protection in the time of danger.

"2). Marion had a strong confidence in me for her own safety and I considered her own wish to return to her father Saturday morning too deeply. However, my desire to secure the money and return to college was even greater. I knew that if I refused to take her back Saturday morning she might distrust me enough to give some sign which would cause my discovery. Yet I felt that if I did take her back in daylight I might fall in a trap and be caught. So in order to go through with my plans enough to get the money and keep Marion from ever knowing why she lived that I would disappoint her confidence in me, I killed her so suddenly and unexpectedly, or she passed beyond consciousness so quickly and unexpectedly that she never had a fear or thought of her own death. Then in order to get her out of my apartment without notice I was prompted after she was beyond consciousness to dissect her body.

"3). For several years I have had a peculiar complex. Even though my habits have always been clean and although my high school record is commendable I have had an uncontrollable desire to commit a great crime. This peculiar feeling, and I believe that it borders on the edge of insanity or that it comes as a weird relief from seriousness or deep thought, found a means of expressing itself in the Parker case. I am very sensitive and have a strong sense of pride. I have not been able to find a real practical value in religion or enough satisfaction that is based on absolute reason. My deep thought on this subject and my apparent disappointment with my conclusion have shaken my sense of morality. However, I do not believe that I am insane or crazy, yet I do think that this complex of mine should not be considered least among my motives in this crime. The fact that a young man is willing to commit a crime to secure expenses through college and especially to a church school helps to explain this complex of mine. I cannot understand it myself but I do consider it a big motive in this crime. I do not consider crime seriously enough. I think that if I want something no matter what means I have to use to secure it, I am justified in getting it. My record of crime illustrates this statement very thoroughly. Even in the murder of Marion

Parker I could not realize the terrible guilt: I felt that some kind of Providence was guiding me and protecting me in this whole case. These facts, I believe, are associated with my complex.

"I want to make a statement here to avoid any suspicion that during my connection with Marion Parker I took any advantage of her femininity. I can only give my word that I did not, but I give this very sincerely and truthfully. My word is substantiated by the doctor's examination of the girl's body and I feel that everyone can be assured that the girl was not molested in any way. I would like to say that I have had no bad personal habits. I have never been drunk or taken any intoxicating drinks. I do not gamble. I have never been in any corrupt conduct with the female sex. In support of these statements reference can be made to my record in the juvenile court of Los Angeles.

"In giving these motives I have been as honest as I know how. I have searched my mind and impulses under all the circumstances and this is my truthful summary.

"William Edward Hickman"

Both of Hickman's statements became widely published in newspapers across the country. The public was alternately fascinated, outraged, and repulsed by the comments from this fiend who killed and dismembered twelve-year-old Marion Parker. Marion had already been given a tragic infamy, and a shocked, vengeful nation waited eagerly for justice to be served.

The detectives noticed how Hickman relished writing his accounts, carefully choosing the correct words just as he had in his debate contests. He wrote, rewrote, added addenda, and carefully worded his account so that it appeared insightful and intelligent. He was proud of the finished product.

One of the writers covering this story was Edgar Rice Burroughs, creator of the popular Tarzan books that were just beginning to be made into motion pictures with Elmo Lincoln in the role of the jungle man. Of course, the Tarzan motion picture series would really take off when Olympic swimming champion Johnny Weissmuller took over the role in 1932 with the MGM feature *Tarzan the Ape Man*.

Burroughs, reporting for the *Los Angeles Examiner*, called Hickman "a moral imbecile" and stated that he was "a new species of man . . . differentiated by something other than anatomical divergences."

There were also editorials trying to blame the media for Hickman's crime. Just as comic books, rock-and-roll music, and television would be blamed in later decades, the motion picture industry came under fire from the era's sob sisters. Hickman's love of the movies had become well known via press reports. So an argument as to cinema's influence on the killer ensued.

An actual meeting was held in New York to debate whether the motion picture industry should undergo federal supervision. Now, in order to understand how preposterous this is, one must realize what type of movies were being made in 1927–1928. Talking pictures were brand new. Al Jolson had sung a few songs and spoken a few lines in the Warner Bros. feature *The Jazz Singer* in 1927. Otherwise, the film was largely silent. It would not be until well into 1928 that an all-talking movie, *The Lights of New York*, would be released. Sound film was very much in its infancy.

The comedy of Charlie Chaplin, the swashbuckling adventures of Douglas Fairbanks, the thrills of Harold Lloyd, the technique of Buster Keaton, the romance of Greta Garbo and John Gilbert, and the early cartoons of Walt Disney were filling the screens. It was more than forty years before movies would have a rating system. Many drawing room dramas, like latter-day soap operas, paid attention to melodrama, with overplayed gestures from stage-trained actors who hadn't mastered the intimacy of the motion picture camera. Slapstick comedy entertained with wild pratfalls and remarkable acrobatics.

The silent film evolved from a storefront oddity to a cultural art form, and the end of 1927 had perfected it. That year offered such timeless classics as *The Kid Brother*, *The General*, and *Sunrise*. When revisiting these exceptional examples of early cinema, it is difficult to understand how they could be considered at all dangerous, much less have enough of an impact to be even remotely connected to the psyche of a murderer like William Edward Hickman.

Hickman loved movies. He also loved opera. To state that his movie fandom had any impact on his gruesome actions is to also indicate that the often-violent operas were as responsible. There was no noted group trying to ban opera as dangerous. However, there was Canon William S. Chase, who was the subject of a *New York Times* article that stated,[2] "The motion picture screen for the past twenty-five years has been a school of crime, according to Canon William S. Chase, who took the informative in debate at the Ingersoll Forum last night on 'Should There Be Federal Supervision of Motion Pictures?' Dr. Wolf Adler upheld the negative. 'Did you notice that in his account of his dreadful crime, Hickman said it was his habit to see motion pictures daily?' Canon Chase asked. He said the movies were a menace to the children of the world, and to the furtherance of world peace. By representing American life in a false light, he charged that motion pictures aroused the antagonism of other countries and created much ill feeling by portraying foreigners as villains and Americans as heroes. Because moving pictures are run by interests with the whole purpose of making money, he urged that the government supervise the movies so as to further the best moral and political interests of the public. Dr. Wolf Adler issued an opposing view by stating, 'If you start censoring motion pictures, you will soon begin regulating literature, the stage, and every other activity of life. The movies do not influence morals for the worse. They merely reflect morals as they are by showing the realities of life. If they are immoral, they are an effect of immorality, not a cause. Federal control will not be of any use because it cannot abolish things as they are.'" It is an argument that, surprisingly enough, still exists in the twenty-first century and has now encompassed all forms of media that have since been created.

During the 1930s, movie gangsters were considered a bad influence on younger viewers. Even actor Huntz Hall, one of the screen's Dead End Kids, stated that all boys wanted to be a gangsters, and "if there hadn't been a war, there would've been machine guns in the streets."[3]

The media have long been blamed when a tangible reason is needed for bad behavior. The fact that the movies of the 1920s were considered enough of a danger to discuss in the same breath as William Edward Hickman and the kidnapping and murder of Marion Parker shows that this argument is very old and has always had little or no real substance.

Along with enjoying movies and music, Hickman seemed to enjoy his celebrity status as a captured killer. At each of the train's stops, there were hundreds of curious gawkers. Hickman would look out at the crowd and try to recognize faces from previous stops. Hickman was pleased that he finally got himself in the movies. Never mind that they were newsreels.

Hickman had resigned himself to having been captured. Now, he felt, it was time to use this situation to his advantage. He was the master

criminal who had committed the crime of the century. He had presented a carefully written account of his crime.

Carlton Williams, a *Los Angeles Times* reporter who was on board
the train covering the journey, referred to Hickman as conceit exem-
plified.

CHAPTER 14

Chief Cline was well aware of the crowds that would likely be meeting the train on its arrival in Los Angeles. He could foresee trouble from a percentage of that crowd since Hickman had become a perverse sort of folk hero. Decadence is nothing new. And just as it seems incomprehensible that one could kill and dismember an innocent little girl, it is just as preposterous that one could generate a gaggle of "fans" for such a hideous act. However, as stated previously, Hickman had his share of supporters, and those supporters could very likely be among the gawkers at the Los Angeles station.

There was also the problem of vigilantism. Hickman did something truly horrible, and the reaction of some would be to kill him just as he killed Marion. Angry crowds can easily evolve into mobs, and there were many that would certainly be ready and willing to lynch Hickman. There could also very likely be a marksman standing quietly among the curious, ready to shoot Hickman down on his departure from the train. Chief Cline would have none of that. He had a plan to sidestep the train station.

The train instead stopped in Alameda, not far from where Hickman had dumped Marion's various scattered remains. Well-armed squad cars met them, and Hickman was quickly whisked away to the Los Angeles County jail, where 4,000 people were waiting. The crowd, as a group, moved toward the killer. Police had to hold back the onlookers with force, including the curious as well as the vigilant. As the guards brought him into the building, Hickman ducked among his burly chaperones, his thin frame guarded from the shouting mob.

Hickman was taken to the tenth floor of the jail and fitted with a ball and chain to keep him from attempting escape. He was heavily guarded. Finally, he was jailed in a cell with extra security locks and its own built-in alarm, which was designed for the most extreme criminals.

In less than an hour, Hickman was brought into the courthouse, being faced by Judge Carlos Hardy. Hardy was the same judge who had presided over his counterfeiting trial a year earlier. [1]

"William Edward Hickman, is that your real name?"

"Edward is my name, your honor."

"William Edward Hickman?"

"Yes, sir, your honor."

"Have you an attorney to represent you?"

" No, sir, your honor."

"You are entitled to an attorney before you are arraigned."

The judge was informed that Chief Cline received a telegram from Hickman's mother, Eva, on his arrival in Los Angeles. Mrs. Hickman had secured the services of noted Kansas City defense attorney named Jerome Walsh, later a close friend of fellow Kansan Harry S. Truman. Walsh had left Kansas City for Los Angeles that morning. He would arrive in a few days. Hickman's hearing was postponed until he was with legal representation. On being returned to his cell, Hickman spoke to the press.

Hickman told the newspapers that he was planning to plead guilty despite the advice of his attorney. He further stated that he was ready for the consequences and hoped for a speedy trial. He even agreed to meet with Perry Parker if asked to do so, promising that he would tell him everything in the greatest detail. Hickman's interest in boasting of his exploits extended even to the sorrowful father of his victim. This reaction appalled the reporters.

When one of the reporters brought up Hickman's written confessions, he asked that they not be printed. He was proud of how they were written, and he craved the attention and publicity but was also impossible to predict. He had worded his confessions so carefully, yet now he wanted them withheld from the press. Perhaps he was concerned about his mother or other longtime friends whose opinion of him had been different. Of course, Hickman's confessions were already in newspapers from coast to coast, although most omitted the horrid details of Marion's dismemberment and the disposing of the body.

Eva Hickman was also talking to the press. She insisted that he was only a tool and was convinced that her boy couldn't have thought out such a terrible thing. She continued to believe that Edward was only carrying out the scheme of some directing head. Hickman's estranged father, William, was located in El Paso, Texas. A tough, burly sort, the polar opposite of his slightly built son, Bill Hickman was honest when reporters caught up with him. Showing remorse for Marion's death and none for his son, the elder Hickman stated that he was content to let the law have him, that he should be punished according to his crime.

Perhaps the most interesting portion of the newspaper was a conflict between Chief Cline and Dr. Wagner. The coroner who examined Marion's remains still was not content that she had died as a result of strangulation. Dr. Wagner issued the following statement:[2]

> I understand that Hickman stated that he strangled the little Parker girl. He may have done or attempted to do what he confessed he did, but her death was not primarily due to strangulation. There were no marks of contusion or constriction about the neck, the lungs were not congested, but on the contrary were quite pale and bloodless, the whites of her eyes were not injected, nor was the face bloated when I first saw the remains. There were no signs of a struggle anywhere on the body, no contusions, lacerations, or scratches upon the hands, wrists, or elsewhere. I knew Marion Parker. She was a very nervous child, and when she realized her situation she probably neither slept nor partook of food during those three terrible days, as shown by her empty, constricted stomach, and from her letters written to her parents it would appear that her captor told her he would kill her if not ransomed: therefore, when he applied the towel about her neck, she realized what was about to happen and her heart stopped as a result of fear and exhaustion. Hickman stated that she did not struggle in his first statement reported. There were no indications whatever that he had mistreated his victim and the chemist reported no poisons or anesthetics.
>
> A. F. Wagner

Chief Cline reacted angrily to Dr. Wagner's statement and provided his own counter in the following day's newspaper:[3] "Hickman told some facts verbally. He was afraid to put them down on paper. We did not allow them to become known while the train was on the way from Oregon to Los Angeles for fear it would incite a lynching. No penalty the law will exact is sufficient for a fiend like Hickman. Hanging is far too good for him, and anything short of hanging would be a gross miscarriage of justice."

Cline was not merely feeding material to the press. There was a great deal more to Hickman's actions than what he confessed on paper. Much of it was so gruesome, it would likely have been edited out before his confession was published in the newspapers. Even Hickman's attorneys were unaware of the more gruesome details until they interviewed him in his cell on their arrival in Los Angeles.

Dr. Wagner could have been wrong about Marion's personality when describing her as "a very nervous child." While Marion was a bit shy around strangers, she was far more gregarious than her sister Marjorie. Dr. Wagner could very well have been getting the personalities of the twin girls mixed up.

Meanwhile, Buck Lieuallen and Tom Gurdane continued to take bows for capturing Hickman. Still no reward had come forth, and more claims from others were coming in regularly. It seemed that anyone who had anything to do with Hickman since the murder was coming out of the woodwork and making a claim. Gurdane was philosophical, indicating that he and Lieuallen were police officers and already getting paid for catching criminals.

Theater chains were asking Gurdane and Lieuallen to tour with their account of the crime as a vaudeville act. It was not so far-fetched. A half dozen years later, the father of public enemy John Dillinger would have a similar touring act, making money off his dead criminal son's infamy.

Gurdane and Lieuallen may have put on that they were simply doing their job and that a reward was secondary. But, Lieuallen, admitted, the two were in Los Angeles to collect and were planning to return home on receiving the reward money. So much for the theater tour.

Meanwhile, William Edward Hickman got settled into his Los Angeles jail cell. He would be appointed defense attorneys and analyzed by doctors. There would be no more moving pictures, no more records, and no more books. Hickman was now a prisoner of the city of Los Angeles, and he realized that he would likely be hanged for his crimes.

CHAPTER 15

Hickman's first few days in lockup at the Los Angeles jail were fraught with visits from various analysts. His sporadic behavior, inconsistent attitude, and the fact that he committed a most horrible crime led most nonmedical laypersons to believe that he was insane. However, the doctors who examined Hickman came away with the belief that he was indeed sane. He explained with lucidity his crime and appeared to realize its effect and the ultimate punishment he must face. According to these doctors, his evil act against Marion Parker was just that, and the analysts were willing to testify.

For his part, Hickman did not appear to be putting on a crazy act to fool anyone, at least not at first. He appeared aloof at one point and introspective at another, but his lucidity and understanding of his actions and their consequences were consistent. This led to the doctors' conclusion that he was in control of his mental capabilities.

It was 4:00 a.m. on Thursday when Hickman was in his cell feeling the need to engage in conversation with one of his many guards. In this case, it was jailer Frank Dewar. He asked Hickman if he had killed anyone else. Hickman made no attempt to cover up his previous crimes. He asked if the guard remembered the druggist at Rose Hill who was shot on the previous December. Indeed, Hickman and his younger accomplice Welby Hunt had pulled a string of robberies in December 1926. Ivy Thoms was shot and killed in the cross fire during one of those robberies. His killer was thought to still be at large.

Hickman was apparently ready to spill everything he had ever done
as a small-time criminal. He asked for a pen and paper and proceeded
to write down the details of this crime, including the cop on the beat
who wandered in during the holdup and was wounded amid the gunfire
as Hickman and Hunt made their escape. Dewar immediately got Hickman's written confession to the homicide department, and a short time
later, Welby Hunt, now sixteen, was picked up on suspicion of murder.

Hunt might have been worried. He should have been. Hickman was
all over the newspapers regarding the Marion Parker murder. Would he
confess to the other criminal activities in which he was involved and
implicate Hunt? Such possibilities had to be running through Hunt's
mind.

Hunt admitted to being a part of the holdup but insisted he had not
fired a shot. He stated that he was carrying a .38-caliber gun, and
Hickman was carrying a .32. Hickman corroborated Hunt's story. After
some investigating, it was discovered that Thoms had been killed with a
.38-caliber bullet. Welby Hunt had inadvertently implicated himself
and was now part of the Hickman case. Some even believed he might
have been an accomplice in the murder and dismemberment of Marion
Parker. But Hickman continued to insist he had acted alone and that he
had no contact with Hunt by that time. Wisely, detectives realized that
Hickman would not likely implicate Hunt in one murder and shield him
from another.

Welby Hunt's mother told the press,[1] "I know my son is innocent.
He is a good boy, and I am certain this merely is Edward Hickman's
means of retaliating. From the very first, when reports came from California that my son had given aid to the police, I was afraid of what
Hickman might do. At first I was afraid he might return to kill my boy as
he killed Marion Parker. Then, when he was captured, I thought my
boy would be safe. But now I see I was mistaken."

Hunt's mother defended her son in the press the way Eva Hickman
had defended Edward. But Edward had confessed to both crimes and
had named Welby Hunt, and now it would be up to the courts to
decide.

Hunt and Hickman had also been together at the time of Hunt's
grandfather's suicide. There had always been some skepticism as to the
suicide notes that A. R. Driskell had left behind. An investigation of
Driskell's death was soon under way.

A handwriting expert went over Driskell's suicide notes. There was a series of tangible similarities between these and the notes Hickman sent to Perry Parker during his abduction of Marion. Perhaps Driskell had not committed suicide at all.

When Perry Parker had first known Edward Hickman as a page at the bank, he found him rather benign until Hickman became involved in counterfeiting. Parker had already recalled to the press the calm demeanor that Hickman displayed when told that he was discharged. Parker compared that with the attitude Hickman displayed during his dealings with him over the ransom and Marion's safety. Parker had stated that he never would have felt Hickman would be a danger to his family.

Little did he realize that Hickman might have already killed two people by the time he worked at the First National Bank. This benign page was noticing Parker, noticing Marion when she visited her father at the workplace, and hoping to someday "commit a great crime," possibly a kidnapping.

Now the press exploded with accounts of Hickman's past. As he casually told of his exploits and wrote them down, they were absorbed by the nation's newspapers and printed for all to read. Edward Hickman was a small-time stickup man. Edward Hickman was already a murderer before even meeting Perry or Marion Parker. Edward Hickman acted alone in the murder of this innocent twelve-year-old child. Edward Hickman was deemed sane by a group of prison psychiatrists.

Hickman was not popular with the other prisoners. A photograph of Hickman was suspended from his cell door by a string. The head on the photo had been cut around, and a cord was attached as a hangman's noose. Hickman remained under heavy guard. Broom handles were broken off by several prisoners and hidden as clubs, with Hickman their intended victim. The weapons were confiscated before anything happened.

Whenever Hickman was escorted past another cell and he made eye contact or flashed his smirk at other prisoners, they glared at him with the same murderous intensity as any of the gawkers at the train station. Unlike many of the townspeople who met the train, these prisoners were fully capable of committing murder, and police realized that Hickman needed to be heavily guarded at all times.

Hickman was admittedly fearful and decided to pen a note to his mother to take his mind off of his immediate surroundings. It was his first communication with her since his capture. He wanted to console her while at the same time still boast about his "crime of the century."[2]

> Dear Mother,
> I certainly appreciate your kind letter and I want you to know that I still care for you. It's so sweet of you to be willing to help, no matter what has happened, and your love is simply overwhelming. I have no fear of what may come. I have been truthful and confessed everything. Everyone has treated me nice. I have slept well and feel in perfect health. In spite of everything people can't help but sympathize with me and praise you for your strong mother love. After talking with me and being around me, people can't realize my guilt, but it is so, nevertheless. Mr. Gustave R. Briegleb of St Paul's Presbyterian Church gave me a Bible and I am reading it some. I like the Psalms and seem to get real comfort out of them. God bless you, Mother. May He comfort you and see the whole thing through to the end.
> Your son,
> Edward Hickman

Jerome Walsh was nearing Los Angeles. Hickman's attorney would soon be aiding the killer of Marion Parker using the same insanity defense that Clarence Darrow had successfully used for Leopold and Loeb a few years earlier. Hickman and Welby Hunt were indicted by a grand jury for the murder of druggist Ivy Thoms. Thoms's widow identified them in a lineup. Hickman again pleaded insanity. Hunt said nothing. At age sixteen, he could not be executed for his crime. Hunt would instead face life in prison. However, Hickman now had two murders that could send him to the gallows.

The Reverend Russell M. Brougher of the Baptist Temple in Brooklyn made the New Year's Day 1928 *New York Times*[3] with a sermon that accused judges of too much leniency:

> There is a spirit of lawlessness influencing nearly everybody. New York, the largest city in the world, naturally would have a very high percentage of crime and yet I believe we have a good Chief of Police. He is handicapped in many ways, but I believe he and his fellow officers are endeavoring as best they can to enforce the law. No

doubt the judges are to blame many times for showing too much leniency in regard to bail and probation. The delay in trying cases and the uncertainty of justice because of the schemes of designing lawyers, and the influence of outside organizations have aroused resentment on the part of the people when heinous crimes have been committed. We expect too much of police officers without giving them our assistance. Many people break the traffic laws and then expect to be excused for doing so. Many people break the prohibition laws and think they ought to go unpunished. There is a spirit of lawlessness influencing the population.

He blamed the judges and judicial system for frequently showing too much leniency in regard to bail and probation. Brougher stated that the delay in trying cases and the uncertainty of justice because of the schemes of designing lawyers and the influence of outside organizations have aroused resentment on the part of the people when heinous crimes have been committed. The reverend called the Hickman capture a great blessing to humanity.

The judge's New Year's sermon was printed in the *New York Times* and helps to reflect the general attitude about crime and criminals, especially in reference to the Marion Parker murder, as the Roaring Twenties was drawing to a close. Of course, at this time, nobody would have predicted the 1929 stock market crash that led to a nationwide Depression that affected most of the country—when bank robbers would become folk heroes and the names of William Edward Hickman and Marion Parker would fade into the dim recesses of the public's mind.

CHAPTER 16

As Hickman's defense attorney, Jerome Walsh from Kansas City, arrived in Los Angeles, prosecutor Asa M. Keyes was gathering more and more data to convict Edward Hickman. Doctors who analyzed Hickman stated that they felt he exhibited sanity in his responses to their questions regarding the murder and dismemberment of Marion Parker.

Dr. Thomas Orbison was one of a battery of psychiatrists who analyzed Hickman. He came away believing that Hickman's sex life was "perfectly ordinary" and made note of the dichotomy between Hickman's professed religious beliefs and his actions. He stated that there was an early conflict between Hickman's religion and criminal instincts and that he chose the criminal side of it. Hickman said as much to Dr. Orbison, offering no reticence or any hesitation about it. Hickman, however, bristled when Orbison asked him his reasons for dismembering Marion Parker. He felt that if he answered these questions the way they wanted him to, it would be used to build up the case of the prosecution. Hickman avoided any questions that could be incriminating. His debate skills were actively responding to the doctor in a manner that would allow him to come off in the manner that he wanted depicted.

For someone who professed insanity, such instances displayed some rather clear thinking on the part of Edward Hickman. It was considered by some that his ploy was to appear like an insane person trying to seem that he was sane. It was a bit convoluted, but Edward felt he could manipulate the system successfully just as he believed his oratory skills could net a national prize. To Hickman, this was just another debate contest. However, aside from this superficial bravado, there were times when Hickman was resigned to facing the gallows. Certainly, his defense attorneys felt that anyone who could commit so horrible a crime as the murder and dismemberment of a twelve-year-old child was most certainly insane. And it was up to these attorneys to prove to a jury that insanity is what drove Edward Hickman to murder Marion Parker.

The barrage of analysts continued. Hickman was more comfortable discussing his sexual feelings and beliefs with another doctor, a Dr. Mikels.

"The first time that I masturbated was about two years ago, after I left high school. The first time I had intercourse was about thirteen years of age. The girl was about twelve. I did this several times while I was in Kansas City."

Hickman also stated, "I don't have any use for whores. Whenever I see a whore, I feel like choking her."

When confronted by Dr. Orbison as to his sanity, Hickman stated, "I don't think I am insane. It was claimed for me."[1]

However, Hickman also continued to write, and he shared his writings with the doctors. Among the things he wrote included a disturbing passage regarding his feelings about the murder of Marion Parker: "The murder of Marion Parker and the horrible, terrible, simply awful mutilation of Marion Parker's helpless body, a separate deed from the kidnapping of Marion Parker, a distinct crime done in blood with a knife by my own hands on the morning of December 17, 1927, in the bathtub in Apartment No. 315 at the Bellevue Arms Apartments of Los Angeles, California, was not mean by me, Edward Hickman, but through me under the guidance and protection of, and as a duty to this great Providence for the great work which it had been calling me since the age of twelve to perform for the safety and security of human rights and liberties in the United States of America."[2]

Hickman had several conferences with his attorney and appeared in the California Supreme Court on January 3 to deliver a plea of not guilty by reason of insanity. Jerome Walsh filed an affidavit asking for delay in entering his client's plea, but this was denied. After Hickman's plea, Walsh again asked for a delay of thirty-five days, which was five days over the state's legal limit. Judge Carlos Hardy noted that Walsh had no probable witnesses in his affidavit and set a trial date of January 25.

There were plans to speed up the jury selection process, the judge considering taking advantage of a new law that would allow him to examine prospective jurors. With Hickman's insanity plea, he was, in essence, admitting to the murder, and thus the burden of proof would be in the hands of his defense attorneys.

Meanwhile, plans were made for Hickman to be tried along with Welby Hunt for the murder of druggist Ivy Thoms. Hunt's attorney had already announced that his client would plead guilty, raising the speculation that Hunt may agree to testify against Hickman. The attorney also intended to have the sixteen-year-old Hunt tried in juvenile court, but the case was referred back to superior court. A trial date for Hunt was set for January 10. Word came through Walsh that Hickman's mother, Eva, and his seventeen-year-old sister, Mary, would be arriving from Kansas City to assist in the defense. Colonel Charles E. "Cap" Edwards would also be among the defense witnesses. The former chief of police of Kansas City had continued to be an adviser to the Hickman family.

Perhaps the most startling news was that Hickman's father, William Thomas Hickman, was planning to come to Los Angeles and aid in the defense of the son he had condemned to the press only days before. Initially shocked by the Marion Parker murder, William Hickman Sr. was content with letting the law take care of his son, telling the press that Edward should pay the extreme penalty. However, after pondering the situation, Hickman Sr. had a change of heart. He stated that his son was undoubtedly insane and requested to be called as a witness at Edward's sanity trial. He believed that he could offer solid evidence regarding his ex-wife's family history that would clearly indicate that Edward was indeed insane and that his insanity plea was not merely a ploy to stay alive. Prosecuting attorneys said that they would demand the death penalty. The defense would work to prove their insanity claim and save Hickman from the gallows. Attorney Jerome Walsh stated that all he sought to do was to find some humane and civilized solution to this tragedy.

As Hickman was being arraigned in the Marion Parker case, he sat next to Walsh, looking down at the floor and speaking only twice, briefly. After entering his plea, Hickman was asked if he knew that his insanity plea constituted an admission of the killing. He responded in the affirmative. At the rear of the courtroom sat Perry Parker Jr. He was the sole representative of the Parker family at the arraignment. He was laying eyes on Hickman for the first time as reporters closely watched the Parker boy's reactions. Parker appeared to be very tense and under a tremendous amount of strain. Reporters recalled that his eyes nervously darted between the judge and the man who killed and dismembered his beloved little sister. When the arraignment ended and Hickman was taken from the room, Parker offered no comments to the reporters who clamored around him and shouted out questions. He left the courtroom without saying a word to anyone.

The newspapers reported that the insanity hearing of William Edward Hickman would be the probable beginning of a long legal fight by the youth's counsel to save him from the gallows. Prosecuting attorneys had frequently declared that they would demand the death penalty for Hickman.

The prosecution had already announced that Marion's long-suffering father, Perry Parker Sr., would be participating in the trial for the prosecution. Perry Parker was not relishing this. His beloved daughter was dead, she would not be coming home, and her killer was in police custody. Parker simply wanted the American judicial system to do what it was meant to do and sentence William Edward Hickman to death.

But Parker realized the importance of his testimony. He would not be cross-examined, and he could be brief and to the point. Parker mulled it over for a long time and talked it over with his son, still protecting his wife and daughter from most of the details. After a long period of conflicting thoughts and serious pondering, Perry Parker agreed to testify against William Edward Hickman for the second time in his life. This time it was for something much more serious than counterfeiting at the bank.

CHAPTER 17

Hickman's attorney, Jerome Walsh, was not working alone. He was working with Richard Cantillon, a defense lawyer who recalled the horror he had felt on first reading of Marion Parker's brutal murder. Cantillon had a child of his own and another on the way. He could not fathom the anguish that Perry Parker was experiencing. Cantillon also believed Hickman could not possibly have been sane. He believed that the very act of killing and dismembering a little girl was reason enough to suppose insanity and to make sure Hickman's rights were not violated. In this modern era, we often hear of situations where it appears that the perpetrator is perceived as another victim. Cantillon's reaction to Hickman shows that such a perspective is not new to the judicial system.

On being hired to work with Walsh, Cantillon announced to the press that he was asking for a change of venue. "All Los Angeles County are biased and prejudiced against the defendant," he said.[1] Of course, virtually everyone in the nation had the same prejudice against Hickman, but still Cantillon felt that Los Angeles County was the worst possible venue for his client. Walsh agreed with him. Cantillon entered the court on January 13 with a request that the trial be held elsewhere. He failed in his attempt to do so, just as attachés of the district attorney's office had predicted. The trial would be held in Los Angeles. A date had been set for January 25.

Hickman himself was exhibiting symptoms of nervous behavior on a far grander scale than before. His nights were sleepless, his body restless. He would sometimes pace the floor until the wee hours of the morning, then collapse in his bunk exhausted. He continued to be heckled by other inmates and was made to feel uncomfortable by the guards. Hickman did not share whatever he might have been pondering as he paced his cell. Was he experiencing remorse? Fearing the eventual outcome? Was his active mind plotting to carefully exhibit behaviors that would land him safely in an institution and avoid the gallows?

Hickman's fellow prisoners were reported in the press as being threatening toward him. Jailers had to keep Hickman constantly behind barred cell doors. According to the *Los Angeles Times*,[2] "Mutterings in prisoners' row reached a climax when a photograph of Hickman was suspended from the accused youth's cell door by a string. The head of the photograph had been cut around and a stout cord tied about the neck with a hangman's knot. Some of the prisoners recently fashioned clubs from broom handles and were holding them in readiness when the improvised weapons were discovered. Jailers did not attempt to conceal their apprehension for Hickman's safety, and plans were in consideration for placing heavier guards about his cell."

Hickman had his legal counsel on his side, and both Walsh and Cantillon were undaunted. After losing their plea for a change of venue, they decided on another avenue to delay the January 25 trial. They spent the next ten days researching every aspect of the case, including findings by various doctors as to Hickman's state. As part of their research, Walsh and Cantillon interviewed Hickman extensively. Edward provided all of the details he had told to Chief Cline, including those that were not printed in his noted confession. During one of the defense attorney's jailhouse visits, Hickman told Richard Cantillon more about Marion's reaction to being kidnapped.

According to Hickman, Marion enjoyed it at first, thinking of her abduction as an adventure. Hickman gave her candy bars and let her play his phonograph. He had a rather impressive collection of then-modern jazz and popular recordings. One of his records, *Pretty Baby*, was her favorite song, and she played it often, sometimes several times in a row. During this period, Hickman grew to like Marion. Marion was indeed a very likable child. She was cute and had personality and a good sense of humor. Hickman found her delightful, and he was enjoying her company.

This was the proverbial honeymoon period. Neither Marion nor Hickman truly concentrated on the situation. To Hickman, this was a major crime that would net him the coveted $1,500 for seminary school. The girl was easily nabbed, she was not a bother, an exchange would be made, and he would get away. To Marion, it was enough of an adventure to keep her from stopping to realize the danger she was in. It was daylight, she was not being mistreated, and it had been promised that by evening she would be back at home. She didn't concern herself with the ransom or her family's worries. She had candy bars, records, and the promise of returning home by nightfall. Everything seemed to be okay on the surface. There was no need to venture any deeper.

The day after the failed Friday night exchange, however, when Hickman noticed police nearby, Marion no longer perceived her abduction as a lark. Hickman had been promising her that if she cooperated, she would be home with her family Friday night. She had, indeed, cooperated, but the police were spotted nearby. Hickman could not make the exchange without getting arrested. The idea was thwarted. But Marion was a child who wanted her parents. It wasn't an adventure anymore. Promising a child something and not delivering will naturally cause the youngster to become upset. Marion wanted to go home and began to cry.

Marion was no longer the cute, likable child whose company Hickman had been enjoying. She was now angry, frightened, confused, and impatient. All of these qualities made her far less interesting. She was now a bother to Hickman. Her crying often neared hysteria, and Hickman was unable to console her. The record player and candy bars were no longer successful. Playing her favorite *Pretty Baby* on the Victrola was only drowned out by her wailing sobs.

Marion demanded through her tears that she be taken home. Hickman tried to be patient and reason with her that if he made the exchange, he would be arrested. Marion would have none of it. She kept insisting, loudly and through tears, that Hickman take her to her house and then just leave her and her family alone. Forget about the ransom, forget the police, and just leave her at her home and drive away. It wasn't interesting anymore. It was scary. Marion was relentless, and Hickman's patience was spent. Marion refused to eat and spent virtually all of Saturday crying. When she finally fell asleep Saturday night, it was due to exhaustion.

The account of Marion's final night also differed from Hickman's written confession. He had written that Marion was tied comfortably with her full knowledge and blindfolded while he prepared to deliver the next note to her father. He also wrote that she asked him to "hurry back." It was then that the intention to kill her completely gripped him. But according to what he told Cantillon, this was not the case. His original confession on the train and carried in the newspapers had altered the true story considerably.

Hickman did not leave a comfortable, unknowing child who promised to be quiet. He admitted to his lawyers that he lifted her sleeping body and put it into a chair, tied her tightly, shoved a handkerchief into her mouth, and gagged her with a dish towel so she could not scream. Marion woke up as she was being bound and tried in vain to scream and struggle. Hickman then shut off all the lights and left her alone, tightly bound and gagged, in his pitch-dark apartment while he sent another letter to her father.

When Hickman arrived home, Marion was screaming through her gag, having trouble breathing, and struggling to free herself. Her eyes were wide with fear. Feeling reproached by the child's terrified eyes, Hickman claimed that he actually felt some immediate remorse at this point. He very briefly considered freeing Marion, returning her home by dropping the frightened child off in front of her house as she insisted he do, and fleeing to another part of the country. But he feared that she would immediately begin screaming on being dropped off and that he would then be caught be police surveying the area of the Parker home.

Hickman wanted the $1,500 in ransom money for his college tuition. He wanted to become a minister. He felt that it was a calling from God. He didn't know what to do about Marion and prayed for guidance. Suddenly, Hickman hallucinated, seeing the vision of an old man commanding him to strangle Marion. "Strangle her," the vision demanded, "strangle her!" Hickman became enveloped in his own hallucination. He felt that it was Providence and that he must obey. While describing this, he even asked his shocked attorney, "If God asked you to do something, wouldn't you do it?"[3]

Hickman stood behind Marion and untied the dish towel that was gagged around her mouth. Marion looked up at him with trusting eyes, and her body relaxed. She apparently believed that she was about to be freed. Perhaps she felt that Hickman was finally going to drop her off at home and leave her family alone forever. Children had imaginations, and Marion could very well have believed that this would all end satisfactorily. It had been a lark until the botched exchange. Now she was upset, bound and gagged, and left alone in the dark. Was it finally over?

Hickman remained helplessly gripped with control by his hallucinatory image. He lowered the dish towel around the child's throat and pulled both ends with all of his strength. The handkerchief he had stuffed into Marion's mouth popped out. There were some muffled sounds of struggle before her body went limp. Hickman then sat on the couch and stared at the child's stillness. Marion remained bound to the chair as the sun began to rise. He pondered what to do with her body.

CHAPTER 18

Richard Cantillon sat dumbstruck at Hickman's description of the murder. It was more than had been included in his much-publicized written confession. While the confession that the newspapers printed had already offered what had happened, Edward refrained from including the more gruesome details. Even the description he offered to his attorneys regarding tying Marion up and leaving the apartment differed from the noted confession that had been carried by the nation's press.

Cantillon realized that he was hearing the details that Chief Cline had alluded to when he stated that no penalty the law will exact is sufficient for a fiend like Hickman. And some of these details had not even been shared with Cline. He got another story, also gruesome but not at this level. Hickman had now revealed that Marion was not comfortable throughout the ordeal as he had originally claimed.

But Hickman's offering of details had just begun. There was more to tell. Now he was ready to offer a more graphic account of the child's dismemberment. And, as the story continued, the details became more gruesome and horrifying. As Hickman calmly explained to his attorney the process by which he intended to cover up his crime, no details were spared. This was not the mainstream press. This was a private conversation with his lawyer, and Hickman knew that he had to tell everything. Perhaps he was even aware of how the heinousness of his subsequent procedure might have helped solidify his insanity defense. Richard Cantillon continued to listen to his client's disturbing account of how he "disposed of the evidence."[1]

While Marion's body lay in his apartment, Hickman cleaned himself up and went to purchase makeup and lipstick. The girl at the counter was amused and asked what a man could possibly want with women's cosmetics. Hickman smiled and but did not answer her. When he returned to his apartment, he pondered the different possible ways he could effectively dispose of Marion's body. The only container he had was a large suitcase. He realized that in order for Marion's body to fit into that suitcase, it would have to be dismembered. Hickman thought for a few more moments and finally concluded that cutting up her body and fitting it into the suitcase was his best option. His approach was very cold and meticulous, as if he had no regard that this was an actual human body, the body of a little girl. Right now, it was merely a mass of matter that he needed to dispose of completely.

Hickman untied Marion's body and placed it on the couch. He used a golf club to measure the length, width, and depth of the body and did the same for the suitcase. He then stripped Marion's body of her clothing and placed the body face down in the bathtub. Hickman tied some towel strips around Marion's ankles, hoisted her body upside down over the tub's drains, and tied the towel to a towel rack. As Marion's lifeless body hung naked over the tub, Hickman harked back to his job on a poultry farm where he disemboweled and disjointed chickens. It was this experience that helped him dismember the child. Hickman pulled on Marion's hair, her head stretched back. With a sharp butcher knife, he cut her throat, slicing through the jugular vein. He then turned on the bathtub water. As the blood drained from Marion's body, a hungry Hickman went into the kitchen and ate a snack of sardines and crackers. When Hickman returned to the bathroom, he placed the body onto the floor, cut into the abdomen, and removed the viscera. He vomited from the odor of the entrails.

After wrapping the viscera in newspaper, he put the torso in the tub and carefully washed out the carcass. He cut the lower part of the torso through the backbone. As he did this, the body jerked with such force that it flew out of the tub. This was later pointed out as a possible indication that life had not completely left the body. Hickman washed the blood from Marion's hair and wiped the torso dry. When he brought the upper portion of the body into the bedroom, he had to cradle the head so it would not become detached.

Hickman had plenty of newspapers. He had bought them all in an effort to read about the kidnapping and how he was being described in the press. Thus, he had more than enough newspapers in which to wrap the body parts. In five bundles, Hickman tied each leg, each arm, and the lower torso. They were placed in his bedroom closet alongside the wrapped viscera. He returned to the bathroom and washed out the bathtub. Then he took a bath.

Hickman slipped Marion's dress over the remains of the head and upper torso. The color had already drained from her face due to the loss of blood. This is where the cosmetics that Hickman purchased came in handy. He carefully applied rouge, lipstick, and powder to register some semblance of pigment to her skin. He then pierced the upper eyelids with a needle, inserted very thin wire that was nearly invisible, and hooked it over the outside of the lid. The eyes were sewn open. But this act was not done with haste. Hickman was very careful not to lift the child's lids so high that she would be exhibiting what appeared to be a frightened look. Hickman sewed the eyelids just above the pupil so that it would appear Marion was alive and awake but just exhausted.

Marion's hair was put into a ponytail; her hair ribbon was steamed and held against a lightbulb to appear newly pressed. A bow was neatly tied around the ponytail. Hickman had carefully created Marion's appearance as if she was a piece of artwork. He realized that it would be dark when he met with Perry Parker and felt that his handiwork would give the appearance that she was still alive. He figured that Parker would ask to see her before handing over the money.

She was ready for delivery.

Marion Parker.

The Parker Twins, Marion (left) and Marjorie with their mother Geraldine.

Perry Parker, Marion's father.

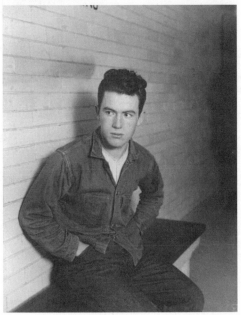

William Edward Hickman.

Hickman's defense attorney Jerome Walsh.

Eva Hickman, Edward's mother.

Letter written by Marion and sent to her parents by her kidnapper.

CHAPTER 19

Richard Cantillon was disgusted by the hideous account that his client, William Edward Hickman, had offered in graphic detail as to his murdering and dismembering of Marion Parker. There were no further details to offer regarding the exchange with her father. All of that had already been known in full detail. Only Hickman, however, could offer an account of what he did following that exchange, when he became a fugitive before his identification and eventual capture.

After murdering and dismembering Marion and delivering a portion of her body to her father in exchange for $1,500 ransom, Hickman returned to his apartment. The place was in disarray. Broken golf clubs were strewn about. It was generally messy, but Hickman wasn't interested in straightening up. It was time for him to move on.

Marion's favorite record, *Pretty Baby*, still rested on his phonograph's turntable. Hickman stared down at the record and started up the machine. As he turned the Victrola's crank, the record slowly began revolving, finally reaching its maximum seventy-eight revolutions per minute. Hickman played the record while he shaved:

> Everybody loves a baby that's why I'm in love with you,
> Pretty baby, pretty baby,
> And I'd like to be your sister, brother, dad and mother too,
> Pretty baby, pretty baby. [1]

There was a knock at the door. Hickman asked who it was. "Police officers!" was the answer. Hickman surprisingly kept his cool. Asking them to wait a moment, he gathered what remained of the ransom money and put it behind the wall ironing board. He then ran to the bathroom and flushed the toilet. Finally, he opened the door and met by two plainclothes police officials. He apologized, claiming that he had been on the toilet.

The policemen entered the apartment, identifying themselves with their badges. Hickman had registered under the name Donald Evans. Despite accounts that he had been in and out of his apartment all day, he had indeed been home when the police came to call. The officers glanced around at the messy apartment and noticed the broken golf clubs strewn about the floor. They asked what had happened with the clubs. Thinking fast, Hickman smiled and shook his head. "After yesterday, I'm never gonna play that goddamn game again!"[2] The officers laughed with Hickman.

Edward asked the officers what they were looking for. They told him they were searching the apartments for clues regarding the fiend that killed and carved up that little girl. Ed looked at the officers. "Wasn't that dreadful?" They nodded.

The officers then darted their eyes around the apartment, peeking quickly in each room but not spending enough time to examine the contents closely. This was just one of many apartments in which they were looking. It was laid out like all the others. Despite being a little messy, it didn't appear that this lonely little apartment warranted careful examination. This small, harmless-looking single man did not seem the type who would harm another. He was the type who took out his frustrations on inanimate objects, like golf clubs. It was the same innocence and calm manner that had made Mary Holt feel safe to allow this man to remove Marion Parker from school days earlier.

The officers were satisfied. They made only a cursory look through the place, barely spending a total of ten minutes, before deciding to move on. There appeared to be nothing worth examining further in the apartment of this man they knew as Donald Evans. Hickman would tell Cantillon that he felt that this close call was proof that God was watching over him.

As Richard Cantillon listened to Hickman relate this more detailed account of the murder and dismemberment, he realized what such information would do to the already angry public opinion. The truncated statements released to the press were enough for the popular vote to insist on his client's execution. If this more graphic information leaked to the press via the courtroom, it could be disastrous to their case.

Hickman seemed to tell more—and with greater accuracy—each time he recounted the days and nights he spent with Marion Parker. And each time the story was told, it became more gruesome. From this latest, most accurate account, Marion's emotions varied greatly. She was relaxed and easily placated at first, then experienced fear and loneliness. She was a little girl, so she cried.

Now, with this accounting of the police visit, it showed that the disarray of his apartment and the broken golf clubs were not enough for the officers to do much further investigation. They were satisfied that Hickman broke the clubs after a particularly bad day on the golf course. Golf was a frustrating game. And the wooden clubs that were being used back in the 1920s could easily be broken over one's knee, even by a frail weakling like Edward Hickman.

Again, perhaps Hickman felt that the lurid details becoming increasingly more graphic might cause greater proof of his own insanity. But when such graphic details are explaining the murder and dismemberment of a little girl and the perpetrator's lack of remorse and subsequent eluding of the police at the crime scene, public opinion could be quite negative. Juries are made up of the public. Cantillon made a mental note not to let Edward take the stand for himself.

It was now time to prepare for the trial. Hickman's attorneys realized that it would be what constituted a media circus back in 1928. While there were no twenty-four-hour cable stations, the Internet, or any other twenty-first-century technologies to which we have now grown accustomed, the trial of William Edward Hickman would still be carried in as much detail as possible in the nation's press. Each day, concerned American citizens who had been appalled by the murder would want to know just what was in store for William Edward Hickman. Would he be executed? Would he be not guilty due to insanity? The attorneys on both sides would argue his fate. The jury would respond to the evidence.

CHAPTER 20

On January 25, as reporters clamored for good seats to cover the proceedings, Judge Hardy arrived in court, a full hour ahead of schedule. Fifty people waited to be called as prospective jurors. There were 150 seats available for onlookers, but more than 1,000 showed up. Among them was Alfred Hickman, Edward's older brother.

Edward Hickman arrived shortly thereafter. He was escorted from his cell to the courtroom by guards armed with tear bombs to quell any possible demonstration by the curious throng. As he entered the courtroom, he made a brief statement to the reporters. While still preparing to maintain an insanity defense, Hickman once again seemed resigned to his ultimate fate.

"I just want this done and over with. I'll swing, I know."[1]

Richard Cantillon was still pondering his past conversations with Hickman, hearing the more gruesome details about Marion Parker's murder and dismemberment and the next day's search of his apartment when Hickman managed to fool two detectives. He remained convinced that Hickman was insane. He and Walsh were determined to prove this in court. Between conferences with his attorneys on the legal phases of his insanity plea, Hickman received dispensation in the county jail for physical exercise, which his lawyers requested to prepare him for the trial.

Court began at 9:31 a.m. Hickman confessed to the murder, with a plea of not guilty by reason of insanity. This was, at the time, a new California law in which the defendant holds that he is not responsible under the law because he was insane when he committed the crime and did not know the difference between right and wrong. The trial, however, did not proceed as planned. Walsh and Hickman made another request that forced the trial to be adjourned until the following day. They filed an affidavit charging Judge Carlos Hardy with prejudice and bias, demanding that a different judge be assigned to conduct the Hickman trial. Walsh made the following charges:[2]

> That Judge Hardy showed prejudice to the defendant when he remarked of Walsh's trip East for depositions that he was "going on a fishing trip."
> That the judge, being presiding judge of the criminal division, showed prejudice when he insisted upon trying the case.
> That Judge Hardy resigned as presiding judge with a prearranged understanding that by such action he would be permitted to sit at the trial of Hickman.
> That Judge Hardy, in his capacity of presiding judge, is bound by the Rules of the criminal branch of the local courts to assign this case, like all others to another judge after hearing the arraignment of the defendant.

Hickman signed and swore to the affidavit in open court, as did Mr. Walsh. Copies were then handed to Judge Hardy and prosecuting attorney Asa Keyes. Keyes characterized the charges as "the most ridiculous thing I ever heard."[3]

Court adjourned until 2:00 p.m. that same day, at which time Judge Hardy spoke to the assembled council. Denying any prejudice against Hickman, Hardy agreed to step down so that another judge could be appointed. Hardy stated that under California law, defense and prosecution counsel were authorized to agree on a judge. Prosecuting attorney Asa Keyes refused to meet with the defense counsel because he disagreed with their charges against Hardy. But Hardy was interested in justice and speeding up the proceedings, so he disqualified himself from the trial.

Judge J. J. Trabucco, a visiting judge from Mariposa County, California, was designated. At this time, Trabucco was a thirty-year veteran of the bench. He had come to Los Angeles to help clear the congested calendar in the local superior court. Now he was about to preside over what was already being called the trial of the century.

The issue of the trial was not whether Hickman killed Marion. That had been established by the insanity plea. Hickman had submitted a signed confession and followed it up with even more gruesome accounts, the latest to his defense attorney, Richard Cantillon. This trial was solely to determine Hickman's sanity on committing the gruesome act. It had to be shown conclusively, beyond a reasonable doubt, that he did not know right from wrong. It had to be proven that he did not realize the consequences for his actions. If found sane, he would be sentenced for Marion's murder and eventually put to death on the gallows as per California law at this time. If found insane, he would be committed to a state institution for the rest of his life.

The trial was scheduled to be reopened at 10:00 a.m. the following day, January 26. The public anxiously waited, hoping for justice to be served. Of course, in early 1928, when the talking picture was still a very new phenomenon, there were no courtroom dramas other than what newspapers and radio news programs offered as information regarding actual cases. Of course, some decades later, the fascination with courtroom drama would inspire cable television stations that specialized in presenting actual trials as entertainment. And the public interest was not much different in 1928.

Marion Parker now symbolically represented every child in America who could somehow fall prey to violence and murder. Edward Hickman was the very embodiment of the boogieman, the frightening, despicable creature who rose from the very depths of evil and murdered and dismembered an innocent child. The newspapers leaned heavily on this sort of melodrama to attract the public. The public responded with shock, revulsion, and, ultimately, rage.

Newspapers embraced sensational stories then as today. Newspaper magnate William Randolph Hearst once admitted that the 1921 rape and murder trial involving popular movie comedian Roscoe "Fatty" Arbuckle sold more copies than the sinking of the *Lusitania*. Hickman was not a beloved celebrity as was Arbuckle (Arbuckle was not only acquitted but also received a letter of apology from the jury). But when a child is the victim of so atrocious a crime, the level of infamy increases greatly.

Edward Hickman was perceived by the general public as a monster. The monster was about to go to trial. And, the public hoped, the monster would eventually receive the same fate as little Marion Parker.

CHAPTER 21

"**W**illiam Edward Hickman, stand up."

Hickman, sitting in the courtroom between his lawyers, Richard Cantillon and Jerome Walsh, stood as the judge ordered. The jury was in the box and had been sworn in. Judge Trabucco was on the bench. Hickman's trial was about to begin.

Hickman's attorneys had another problem. The former star of the high school debate team continued to insist that he take the stand in his own defense. Hickman appeared to enjoy the spotlight, however negative. He had wanted to commit a big crime, and since he didn't get away without capture, he seemed to take some solace in receiving all of the negative attention on so grand a scale. It was also determined by various therapists who knew Hickman's backstory that he was, in a roundabout way, trying to avenge his poor showing at the two national debates. With the world at his attention, he wanted to recount his actions regarding Marion's kidnapping, murder, and dismemberment with the same fluency as he had for his lawyers. Already trying to attract attention to his testimony, Hickman even told reporters that he would speak in his own defense, "whether they liked it or not." Of course, his lawyers did not like the idea of his speaking. They felt that it would ruin their attempt to prove him insane.

Hickman's chief defense attorney, Jerome Walsh, countered Edward's statement to the newspapers. "We do not want Hickman to take the witness stand in view of his insanity defense, and we have told him so. Of course, if he is determined to talk we cannot stop him, but such a move will seriously injure defense plans."[1]

Hickman believed that the psychiatrists who examined him in his jail cell and who were seated at the front of the courtroom were making observations as to his behavior, catching the attention of the jury. Hickman believed that he should show the court what a good debater he was. He saw the courtroom situation as little more than another debate, the skills in which he took great pride. His having received honorable mention instead of a top prize back in high school still rankled him. He wanted to display his skills in what he considered the ultimate debate: the courtroom. And to be doing it with the world at his attention was too grand of an opportunity for Hickman to ignore.

The attorneys knew that Hickman would not be called on the first day, so they decided to convene and come up with a strategy that would convince Hickman that his taking the witness stand would not be in his best interest. Each time Hickman retold the story of Marion Parker's murder, he added more gruesome details. Presenting the same account in the courtroom as he had told Richard Cantillon, in the same relaxed manner, would certainly affect an already angry public, including the twelve jurors. If the lawyers could do anything at all, they would do everything possible to keep Hickman from displaying his oratory skills on the stand in an attempt at his own defense.

As the trial was about to begin, deputy sheriffs were stationed at the entrances to the courthouse to search spectators for potential arms. There were no metal detectors back then. The deputies had to search each entrant individually. The jail had received many letters threatening to kill Hickman. The law was taking no chances that this trial would be abruptly thwarted by an assassin's bullet.

At the outset of the trial, Judge Trabucco presented the new California law regarding trials about a person's sanity:[2] "Insanity means such a diseased and deranged condition of the mental faculties as to render the person incapable of distinguishing between right and wrong in relation to the act with which he is charged. An irresistible impulse to commit an act, which a party knows to be wrong and unlawful, does not constitute the insanity, which is a legal defense.

"The standard of accountability is this: Had the party sufficient mental capacity to appreciate the character and quality of the act? Did he know and understand that it was a violation of the rights of another and in itself wrong? If he had the capacity thus to appreciate the character and comprehend the possible or probable consequences of his act, he is responsible to the law for the act thus committed and is to be judged accordingly.

"Although it is true that generally the burden of proof is upon the prosecution, yet to this rule there is this exception: Where insanity is relied upon as a defense, the burden of proving the existence of such insanity is on the defendant, and it is incumbent upon him to establish by preponderance of evidence that he was insane at the time of committing the act charged."

For his part, Hickman had been stoic throughout the proceedings as far as the public and the press were concerned. Any emotional disruptions were always exhibited away from the newspaper reporters and the jaded, critical eye of the general public.

The clerk read the indictment aloud:[3] "In the Superior Court of the State of California in and for the County of Los Angeles, Indictment Number 32543 filed December 22, 1927, The People of the State of California, Plaintiff, versus William Edward Hickman, Defendant. The said William Edward Hickman is accused by the Grand Jury of the County of Los Angeles with the crime of murder, a felony, committed at and in the County of Los Angeles, State of California, and before the finding of this indictment as follows to wit: That the said William Edward Hickman, on or about the 17th day of December, 1927, at and in the County of Los Angeles, State of California, did willfully, unlawfully, and feloniously, and with malice afterthought, kill and murder one of the statute in such cases made and provided and against the peace and dignity of the People of the State of California.

"The defendant, Hickman, pleads not guilty by reason of insanity to that charge, and is now before you for trial."

Hickman's stoicism gave way to obvious nervousness. He fidgeted, squirmed in his chair, and would frequently run his finger around the inside of his collar. Meanwhile, the front-row psychiatrists took notes as the jurors looked on. Hickman's ploys would now have to work themselves out in a court of law. It was not another fantasy. Hickman was on trial for the murder of Marion Parker, and his life was now at stake.

As the trial began, many important persons who were involved in the case appeared in court. Mary Holt, the school official who allowed Marion to leave school with Hickman, was among the first. The tremendous stress that she had endured in the past several weeks had caused her to look as if she had aged ten years. She had endured a series of breakdowns and was under a doctor's care. Her attendance at school became sporadic, but the administration sympathized with her. Even the Parker family did not speak out in blame for her lack of judgment in allowing one of the students for which she was responsible to leave the building with a stranger who later killed and dismembered her.

Mary Holt's husband helped her as she slowly approached the bench. She appeared as if she would collapse before reaching her destination, but she made it to the bench and sat down. Maintaining as much composure as she could muster, Mary Holt once again tearfully pointed out Hickman in court, and her quivering voice recounted the day that she made the worst decision of her life. "Oh, I can think of many things I could have done now," she said. "I never would have let Marion go but for the apparent sincerity and disarming manner of the man."[4] She gave as many details as she could. She began shaking and crying. The lawyers and the judge did not question her for long. Once they had finished, she left the courtroom.

The district attorney's chief investigator, George Contreras, was soon on the witness stand, recalling the night he went to Manhattan Place after receiving an urgent call and found a shocked, grief-stricken Perry Parker and the mutilated remains of Marion Parker.

"We searched the automobile and searched the area. When the coroner arrived, I carried the little body out of Parker's car and put it in the dead wagon; then we came down to the morgue with it."[5]

Contreras was a tough guy in the same vein as "Hard-Boiled" Herman Cline. He was normally unshakable. But it took great amount of effort to retain any sense of emotional stability as he recounted the events of that evening when he was the first to arrive on the scene, to see Perry Parker just after his having discovered his dead, dismembered little girl. And he recalled his own first look at Marion, her deadened eyes staring blankly, with the eyelids carefully stitched open. Contreras's toughness was hardly enough to suppress his emotions as he recounted these details.

George Watson, a *Los Angeles Times* photographer, was allowed to act in an official capacity and take pictures for the coroner of Marion Parker's mutilated remains. These pictures were presented in court and offered to the jury for inspection.

The photographs of Marion Parker's dismembered body were more gruesome than any of the twelve jurors could have imagined. Here was the little girl who had gained a certain infamy on her kidnapping and murder. A picture of her playful, smiling face had graced newspapers across the country. Now the jurors looked at the severed limbs, the torso that ended just below the naval, and the lifeless face with the eyes stitched open. Reading about Marion's fate had certainly been unsettling, but it was nothing compared to the enormity of viewing these terrible graphic images. Each of the twelve jurors exhibited shocked, horrified expressions. One of the women fainted. Judge Trabucco adjourned court for the day.

"Bear in mind, ladies and gentlemen, the admonition of this court: Do not talk among yourselves or with anyone else upon any subject connected with this trial, or form or express any opinion thereon, until the case is finally submitted to you."[6]

Meanwhile, one of the doctors who examined Hickman told the press that Jerome Walsh said that Hickman had repudiated his confession. Walsh claimed that he had not discussed that subject with anyone and had not made a statement of any kind regarding a repudiation by his client. Mr. Walsh did reveal his and Richard Cantillon's plans for continuing the fight for Hickman's life should their defense be met with defeat in the accused killer's insanity trial once it resumed the following Monday. Walsh stated that if the jury members in the present trial would find that William Edward Hickman was sane at the time of his crime, an arrest of judgment will be asked, along with a demand for another trial on the plea that the defendant is now insane. Meanwhile, District Attorney Asa Keyes responded to Hickman's alleged disclaimer with an assertion not only that Hickman had admitted his guilt in written and spoken forms but also that his plea of guilty by reason of insanity was itself a direct and legal admission of the facts of the crime.

Hickman's father, William Thomas Hickman, was set to take the stand once the trial resumed. It was an attempt by the defense to show the lineage of insanity among Hickman's family members.

CHAPTER 22

"**W**ill you state your name?"

"William Thomas Hickman."

"What is your address, Mr. Hickman?"

"El Paso, Texas."

"Are you acquainted with the defendant, William Edward Hickman?"

"I am."

"What is the relationship?"

"He is my son."

William Thomas Hickman had initially believed that Edward should be punished to the full extent of the law and said so to the newspapers from his home in El Paso. The senior Hickman felt that Edward's crime was too horrible to contemplate. But here he was in the courtroom, far from his home in Texas, attempting to help the defense prove Edward's insanity.

Since his initial reaction to the press, William Sr. contemplated how a child of his could have committed such a terrible crime. He decided that it was the insanity on Edward's mother's side of the family. Hickman Sr. contacted Edward's lawyers. They were trying to prove him insane. Mr. Hickman felt that he could help save his son from the California gallows.

The trial got under way after a jury of four women and eight men had been completed and sworn in. All the jury members were middle aged or older. Judge Trabucco quickly denied a motion by the defense for dismissal of the indictment against Hickman when counsel for the defendant placed in the record a declaration that they were not dissatisfied with the jury.

Being questioned by Richard Cantillon, one of his son's defense attorneys, William Hickman told of the problems that his ex-wife, Edward's mother, had in regard to her own mental faculties. She had been in asylums and had attempted suicide. She had suffered breakdowns. This was argued as being hereditary.

William Hickman testified that his wife's mother, Edward's grandmother Rebecca Buck, was insane.[1]

"She was of a very melancholy nature," he said, "put in the bigger part of her time crying, it seemed like.

"There was part of the time that she did not know anything. She always imagined that there was something badly wrong with her, and her husband spent hundreds of dollars for medicine and doctor bills.

"It came on up until about six or eight months, I guess, before she died, and then she did take what doctors call a stroke of paralysis; she was partially paralyzed, but she was all the time accusing the neighbors of doing dirty deals and all, and thinking that everybody had it in for her. She would run in the fields at night and yell, mostly in the full of the moon.

"Well, she would steal herself away, and we would have to get out and hunt for her. Sometimes we would hunt an hour or two at a time, and when we would find her, she would be hid someplace, just down crying. And we would ask her what was the matter, and she did not know. That is all we would ever get out of her, she did not know.

"And she imagined part of the time that she had heart failure. She would have what she called smothering spells, but it was nothing more than epileptic convulsions, I always thought. She would drop on the floor and, of course, we would all grab her and put her on the bed and start working with her, and work with her until we could bring her out of that. We would keep her from swallowing her tongue, and loosen all her clothing and wipe her face with warm water.

"Sometimes she would have one or two a month maybe for two of three months. Then, from six months, six or eight months, she would not have them."

After discussing Rebecca Buck, Cantillon asked William Hickman about her husband, Paul Buck, who would have been Edward's grandfather.

"He had been pretty well fixed in his young days and an uncle that he had broke him up; that is, he had a lot of property in Pittsburgh, and his uncle went back to sell out his property and close up his business for him, and when he did he left and went back to Germany, and the old man never did hear from him any more. That is where his money went. He was worth, I guess, 25 or 30 thousand before he lost that; and after that the old man worried quite a bit. He never seemed to get over that entirely."

Cantillon next asked William Hickman about his ex-wife, Edward's mother, Eva Hickman.

"She began just like her mother. She would steal herself out nights and sit and cry, and I would get up out of bed and hunt around until I would find her, and finally bring her in the house and try to console her. And she kept that up for a good many years, until after our second child was born, and then she began to get worse.

"She always had a horror of children, giving birth to children; and married relations, such as sexual relations; she always had a horror to that. That was her one great fault that she always had to me, that I wasn't of the same nature she was. Of course, I was just like any other man. Well, when she became aware of the fact that she was going to be a mother, why she was worse than any other time of the year. Then is when our worst troubles would always start, but I had doctors with her all the time, bought medicine for her and spent everything that I made, outside of just what we could barely have to live on, in that way. Nothing they did was any good up until about the time our third child was born, and then she got worse; in fact she went perfectly crazy at times.

"There were times she would threaten me with everything imaginable. She was going to kill me, kill the children, and kill herself. She always seemed like she wanted to do some great crime or other; I don't know why; and I talked to the doctors about her and they would say, 'Oh well, it is just a nervous breakdown; she will come out of it all right.'"

William Hickman testified that his wife's problems continued until she was pregnant with Edward. She became so unglued that she would threaten to murder her unborn child by "taking a knife and ripping herself open." She would also threaten that she would cut up the children and that William Hickman would arrive home from work and find their bodies piled up in a corner of the house.

Eva Hickman, according to William Thomas Hickman's testimony, was at her worst during the nine months she was pregnant with Edward. She suffered through thirty-six hours of labor before Edward arrived. Stillborn.

"He was dead at the time," William Hickman told the court.

"The doctors worked with him for, it seemed to me like an hour before they brought him to. He was just as black as anything you ever saw. I thought he was gone for good."

William Hickman continued to tell of his wife's suicide attempts, her time in the insane asylum, and the fact that he had left the family when Edward was seven years old.

Attorney Cantillon had completed his questioning. The jurors were concentrating on William Hickman's testimony, and its impact was noticeable. The defense considered William Hickman's testimony beneficial to their case.

Judge Trabucco called a recess until 2:00 p.m.

William Thomas Hickman left the stand and walked slowly out of the courtroom. He had long ago escaped the tension of his marriage and family. He had virtually no contact with his children from that point on. He had even condemned Edward in the newspapers on learning about his involvement in the kidnapping and murder of Marion Parker. Apparently, his traveling to California and speaking in his son's defense did not impress Edward.

As he walked out of the courtroom, William Thomas Hickman stared in Edward's direction, trying to make eye contact with his son. But it was all in vain; Edward remained looking ahead and did not even glance in his father's direction.

CHAPTER 23

After William Hickman's testimony, Edward's attorneys had some concern over the upcoming testimony of Eva Hickman, Edward's mother. William Hickman testified as to his ex-wife's fragile emotional state, causing both Jerome Walsh and Richard Cantillon to wonder if she would be helpful to their case or a hindrance. The unpredictable nature of this woman, as her history was described in court, could hamper their attempt to help her son avoid the gallows. On the one hand, they realized that any display of possible insanity on the part of Eva Hickman could be beneficial in their attempts to prove the same state for Edward. On the other hand, they pondered that perhaps she could be coherent enough to offer instances in which the jury would find it difficult to believe Edward to be insane at the time of Marion Parker's murder. Would lucidity be detrimental to the case?

Walsh and Cantillon met Eva Hickman for lunch and worked hard to impress on her the importance of her testimony to save Edward from the gallows. She seemed to understand and, after spending most of the meal in abject silence, began to respond well to the lawyers' questions. She was not particularly eloquent, but she was clear. She did not embellish, but she did offer enough necessary information. And even when she seemed relaxed and comfortable with the lawyers, there was a discernible underlying jitteriness to her manner that was as compelling as it was disconcerting. Walsh and Cantillon returned to the courthouse with Eva at 2:00 p.m. after the recess had elapsed.

Eva Hickman entered the courtroom with all eyes on her. She was assisted by Richard Cantillon, who took her arm and led her to the area where Edward was sitting with his head bowed. She put her hand on Edward's shoulder. He looked up at his mother. As the two faced each other, they shared a certain glint in their eye, something that was difficult for reporters or later accounts to describe. But everyone in the courtroom noticed. One woman even said aloud, "Oh, my god!" and the bailiff was so engrossed that he did not quiet her with his gavel. Edward seemed to notice this outburst and quickly looked down again.

Suddenly, the judge's voice broke the tension.

"Will counsel direct his witness to the stand?"[1]

Richard Cantillon made a plea to the judge to ask leading questions, a method usually not allowed in a case such as this. Eva Hickman, it was determined, would likely need to be led in order to recall events that were necessary to the case. The judge allowed this, overruling an objection from the prosecution.

Eva Hickman was sworn in and took the stand. Her voice was small, tinny, and shaky as she recounted the mental deterioration that ate away at her mother, Rebecca Buck. She was twice asked to speak up because the jurors could not hear her. Eva's testimony coincided well with her ex-husband's earlier that same day, except that she was able to offer even greater detail to her family's troubles. Jurors were transfixed as Eva Hickman recalled how, as a child, she would carry a lantern while her father searched for her mother in the dark night, with Rebecca Buck's piercing screams as their only guide.

In regard to her own state, however, Eva Hickman had no details. When attempting to lead her in the direction of clarifying her situation with her marriage to William Thomas Hickman and her reaction to him emotionally and sexually, Eva continually responded to lawyer queries with, "I can't recall."

Eva's voice remained weak, with little inflection. The expression on her face never changed. Spectators concentrated carefully on her, but Edward remained with his head bowed, offering no discernible reaction to his mother's testimony.

Regarding Edward, Eva recalled his deep hatred for his father after William Thomas Hickman left the confines of his disruptive family life. She also recalled Edward's eloquence, popularity in school, and success as a teenager in academic and cultural events. She pointed to Edward's losing the oratorical contest as the catalyst for his descent into the madness that eventually led to his petty crimes. Eva Hickman's voice quivered. Recalling the citizen her son Edward had been and the fiend he had now become affected her emotionally. She tried not to show it. But she had more to say.

After the forgery charge, Edward returned to Kansas City in disgrace. He was no longer the master debater and popular high school vice president. He was a common thief whose petty crime had obliterated any of his past accomplishments. Little did the townspeople or his mother know that he had already committed two murders by this time. It was a secret that Edward was able to keep until being arrested for killing Marion Parker.

Eva Hickman ended her testimony by recalling how Edward left home without a good-bye when he eventually returned to California with the idea that he needed $1,500 to enter a religious college and become a minister. She didn't hear from him again until discovering that her son had been charged with the murder and dismemberment of a twelve-year-old child. She learned this information from a newsboy shouting headlines on a Kansas City street corner.

The defense had concluded its questioning, but the prosecution had no questions for Eva Hickman. There was nothing she could offer their case, and she would likely not bear up well during cross-examination. As a result, court was adjourned.

Cantillon and Walsh had plans to examine a series of important depositions that pertained to the Buck family insanity from other family members and close friends. These would be presented to the court the following day.

Eva Hickman left the courtroom slowly, her gray hair tied in a tight bun at the back of her head, stretching her forlorn face. She still had the indescribable glint in her eye as she was gently led through the courtroom and out the door she had come in. Reporters later commented on the discernible look of a lifetime of suffering that was evident in her face. She also appeared to be emotionally drained, indicating that the questioning had taken a great deal out of her.

The mother of Edward Hickman was suffering. The jurors could see that. But it was not enough to make them forget how much more painfully the mother of Marion Parker was suffering over the same crime. As Eva Hickman left the courtroom, all eyes were on her except for Edward's. He was still looking down.

CHAPTER 24

Perhaps the most trying portion of a trial is the series of depositions that are read as evidence. Jurors are quickly and easily bored by such presentations. Richard Cantillon later wrote that his law partner, Frank Sievers, had an exceptional speaking voice and delivery. As a result, his reading of the depositions was capable of keeping the jurors' attention throughout. There was some genuine importance to the deposition indicating the insanity of Edward Hickman's family lineage, including his mother, his maternal grandmother, and his cousin Otto Buck.

The first deposition read was from Thomas Lewis,[1] who was married to Eva Hickman's sister, Minnie. Lewis recalled that Otto Buck, the son of Eva and Minnie's brother John, had suffered from epileptic fits since childhood.

"He was foolish. He didn't have any mind. He talked and acted like a child."

Lewis also indicated how Eva's mother, Rebecca Buck, would range in mood from delirious happiness to gloomy despair with alarming frequency. Her husband, Paul Buck, stubbornly refused to admit to her insanity and took to regular prayer that she would settle into some state of normalcy. Of course, that never happened.

Of Eva Hickman, Lewis stated that her erratic behavior began as she started having children. "Her ways indicated that she acted queer, anything would tear her all to pieces, and she talked foolish." Lewis concluded by stating, "I had a lot of confidence in Edward. If that boy committed this awful crime, he has to be insane. There is no other way of accounting for it."

Eva Hickman was deemed insane in several of the ensuing depositions. It was the opinion of Artie Smith, sister of William Thomas Hickman; Ida Hickman, who was married to William Thomas Hickman's brother; and Mrs. Mae Forrester, who had known Eva Hickman for more than twenty-five years.

There were further depositions from doctors who had attended Eva Hickman. Insanity was the prevailing opinion based on her long crying jags, suicide attempts, and violent behavior toward her husband and children. Each of these depositions was read separately as question-and-answer sessions, with all details contained therein. Sievers's oratory skills continued to maintain the jury's attention.

But there was a bit of a problem with Mr. Sievers's great speaking voice. The prosecution attempted to object to Sievers's delivery, whose inflections appeared to be editorializing the contents of the depositions. But these objections were overruled. The defense continued to present evidence regarding Hickman's family background, continuing to believe that the insanity of Hickman's lineage would lead the jurors to conclude that some genetic quality must have overtaken him when he murdered Marion Parker.

However, during the trial, the prosecution presented its case succinctly. A twelve-year-old girl was killed and dismembered by a fiend whose careful plotting before, during, and after the crime showed that he knew exactly what he was doing. It was pure evil from a truly evil person who was too pragmatic in his approach and execution to not be fully sane.

After the depositions, court was adjourned until Monday morning. On Saturday, Cantillon and Walsh met with Hickman. Ordinarily, Hickman had little to say, but on this day, the lawyers found him to be especially excited.

Hickman once again insisted on taking the stand. The lawyers were shocked. They realized that this could hurt their case and felt that they had effectively convinced Hickman that his testifying was a bad idea. Hickman wanted to exhibit the lucidity that his lawyers were trying to prove to be tenuous at best. He perceived the trial in the form of a debate. One side is presenting something to convince the other side, and the two sides are using their oratory skills to prove their point.

Hickman considered himself an expert at debating. He had won awards. Hickman was still trying to vindicate the loss that had altered his life forever and led him from petty crimes to the murder and dismemberment of a child. Debating for his very life was just too irresistible.

The lawyers were powerless in their attempts to dissuade Hickman from taking the stand. They had their psychiatrist, Dr. Skoog, visit Hickman the following day. Cantillon recalled that Skoog had a real understanding of Hickman's personality. They were right. After a long visit during which Skoog and Hickman had a long discussion, Hickman told his lawyers that he no longer was interested in taking the stand. But this would not be the last time he would bring it up.

When court reconvened on Monday, the jurors heard from many people from Hickman's past. They recalled his popularity and success and also his eventual losing of the oratorical contest that had often been seen as the catalyst that changed his behavior.

Past friends and acquaintances recalled how the bright, likable Hickman became withdrawn and difficult on losing the contest. He decelerated his activities, believing that everyone was talking about him, laughing at him behind his back. This paranoia seeped into his private thoughts to the point where he even started avoiding the people who had once been his closest friends.

One of the more interesting depositions came from James Parker,[2] a thirty-five-year-old former employer of Hickman when Edward worked at a food market killing and dressing live chickens. "He could not kill a chicken. He told me that he just did not have the heart to kill it. I just can't understand what happened to him. He must have gone completely crazy."

Hickman sat quietly listening to the depositions from people who had once been his close friends. They could not believe that the boy they knew turned into the evil man who killed and dismembered a little girl. Hickman offered no discernible reaction, at least not until the testimony of Dr. Skoog[3] was offered the following day. Skoog read, from his own notes, an interview he had conducted with Hickman:

Skoog: Do you consider yourself a Christian?

Hickman: No, sir.

S: What are you, then?

H: I have a power over me that is equal and which is more than God to anybody, but that nobody feels. They have something over them, and they are satisfied, and I am satisfied.

S: I understand you wished to study for the ministry.

H: I read the Bible. I have a New Testament, and I have read Matthew, Mark, Luke, and John. This morning, I read some of the Revelations. I do not care to read the Old Testament; I don't understand it, as it has not much in it for me.

S: Is your reading of the New Testament in conformity with this Power you have over you?

H: Yes, I must know what is in it to preach.

S: What is this Power you have over you?

H: It is a Divine Power. It is Providence.

S: Then it is God?

H: No, it is superior to God; it is different; it does not work the same way.

S: Does anyone other than you have the benefit of this Power?

H: No, sir. It is especially for me.

S: Why should you be different from the others?

H: Well, I know I am different.

S: How long have you felt different?

H: Since I was a young boy. When I first came to the city.

S: What age were you then?

H: When I was 12 or 13 years of age. I have not felt like any of the boys or anyone. I don't think I should feel sorry because I am not the same as other boys.

S: Suppose people were to ridicule you for being, as you say, different?

H: I have been kidded around by lots of people.

S: What did these people think?

H: They were as crazy as I am.

S: Do you think you are crazy?

H: No, I do not.

S: But you just said you were crazy.

H: Crazy has lot different meanings. I have had lots of people call me crazy but I do not believe they meant it. Lots of times you say "crazy" when you just mean queer or silly. But insanity is something I don't understand. I do not believe I am insane, but I am different from other people.

S: You are not different in appearance, are you?

H: No, I feel different. I see things differently.

S: Now, do the other fellows see you as a different individual?

H: They may and they may not. In other words, as far as looks are concerned, I look just like other people do, but they don't know how I feel.

S: Do you think I can distinguish any difference in you?

H: After telling you my secret, you can understand.

S: Is what you told me a sacred secret?

H: Yes, sir, I seldom tell anybody.

S: Are you directed to keep it secret?

H: I can tell you. I told my mother of it. I told my friend, Don Johnstone. I told Mr. Cantillon and Dr. Shelton because they must know to understand me. They are helping me. I told Mr. Moise, a reporter who comes to visit me; he is writing a story about me. I never like to disclose my complete views on it; that is, in trying to explain it, I just haven't words to give the exact idea of it. It talks to me and suggests things. I hear it; I have seen it. Beyond any doubt, it really exists. It has been known to me for a long time. I do not try to overcome this power. It is far greater than I am. I am humble, passive, and obedient to it. It is something I should not try to understand.

S: Can you tell me more about how this Power makes itself known to you?

H: I feel the Power over me. With the aid of this Power, I know I will become great. I never stop to figure it out. If the Power directs me, I do it. I know it will lead to a great end. I think it plans everything for me. It is predestination. All human beings, no matter how smart they are, have only a shade of conception of the universe. But the Power knows all. It is Supreme Greatness. I used the name Providence, but that does not exactly describe it.

S: Do you know of anyone else with whom your Providence communicates?

H: It has not been revealed to anyone else, not even Christ.

S: You say Providence talks to you; how does it sound?

H: It is soft, but powerful. When it is speaking, I cannot move. Chills run down my spine.

S: You have seen pictures of God in white flowing robes. I presume your Providence appears much like God.

H: No, my Providence has fiery eyes; they seem to burn a hole in me.

S: But what robes does it wear? What color?

H: It does not wear robes. It wears a white suit, shirt, tie and shoes. It looks so strong, it frightens me.

S: But why should you be afraid? It is your benefactor.

H: There are things, I told you, I just don't understand

S: But won't your Power reveal these things to you?

H: I think it will be told to me, when it wants me to know. Not until then.

The doctor concluded that Hickman's visions of Providence stemmed from a grandiose delusion that was common in paranoid schizophrenics.

Shortly after Dr. Skoog's testimony, court was adjourned until the following day. As the lawyers were packing up their briefcases, they were approached by a deputy sheriff telling Walsh and Cantillon that Hickman must see them right away.

Cantillon met with Hickman about an hour later. He found a furious man pacing his cell, his eyes wide. It was not the stress of the situation this time. It was anger—the sort of anger that Hickman may have alluded to in his statements but that never presented itself during this ordeal. It was the sort of all-encompassing anger that could, in fact, be dangerous. Cantillon did not feel in danger. This was a prison, and there were armed guards everywhere. But the attorney realized that Hickman's agitated state was serious enough to address. After a few seconds of pacing, Cantillon asked Hickman what was wrong. Hickman began shouting at the lawyer.[4]

"I thought those doctors were my friends! I am going to take the stand and tell the jury they are telling a pack of lies!"

Hickman's sacred secret of his Providence, which he shared with only an intimate few, was broadcast through the courtroom. It would make its way into the newspapers. Hickman was absolutely livid. Something he considered private, special, and even sacred had been revealed as the hallucinogenic ravings of a lunatic. Hickman wanted to plead insanity to save himself from the gallows, but he did not want his spiritual convictions dismissed as craziness.

"Don't you believe me?" Hickman asked Cantillon.

Hickman then fell to his knees and began sobbing from the very depths of his being. The anguished cries racked his body.

"They didn't let me know they would do that!"

Cantillon calmed Hickman down, explaining how the testimony would help their case. He explained that an insanity defense forced them to use what they could in order to prove their claim. It would save him from the gallows.

Finally, Hickman stopped crying and regained his composure. He appeared to realize that his attorneys indeed knew what was best for him and for their case.

This was the second time Cantillon had seen Hickman cry.

It was also the last.

CHAPTER 25

Hickman's tears of hurt were not in evidence when the doctor's testimony continued the next day.[1] Dr. Skoog continued to reveal what Hickman had told him during their sessions. It was part of Walsh and Cantillon's attempt to convince the jury of their client's insanity. They believed that their client's own words were one of the strongest factors in proving Hickman's plea. But they stopped short of allowing their client to testify with his own words. The documents they had from doctors and analysts would better suffice.

When asked to elaborate about his feelings for Marion, Hickman offered some unusual comments:

> Hickman: I think she was actually born and lived for this thing. It is true she may not then have known about it, but she was prepared and brought into this world for this very thing
>
> Skoog: Does she now know about it?
>
> H: I believe she now knows; maybe she always knew.
>
> S: Isn't she angry with you?
>
> H: No, sir.
>
> S: Why isn't she angry with you who took her life away?

H: I killed her. Yes, I murdered her. But I don't think I took her life away.

S: Did Marion ever give you any indication whatsoever that would cause you to believe that she was aware of what would happen to her?

H: She told me that a week before the kidnapping she dreamt that a strange man came to school and took her away. She told me this voluntarily. She said this about seven o'clock the evening of the day I took her away, when we were driving along Foothill Boulevard. She told me that she had several dreams about this before. She said her mother always warned her about getting into an automobile with a strange man. She told me she never thought it would be so bad to be kidnapped. She said that in daydreams at her desk in school she had also imagined this. I felt this was a positive manifestation of this power that I have been trying to describe as having influence over me. It was all prearranged. I feel that there are two shades to this affair. One was Providence bringing me before the world; the other was Providence trying me to see if I was super strong and capable of doing the work. He would set out for me. It was all sort of a test.

Perhaps the most uncomfortable testimony for all involved were the details as to Hickman's sexuality. There had been no evidence that Marion was sexually assaulted. The doctor who examined her remains had testified that there was no indication of such an act. But if Hickman could be so gruesome as to kill and dismember her, wasn't he then also capable of sexual assault?

On this subject, Hickman was adamant. He never took advantage of Marion in that fashion. He never thought of doing so. Hickman was a strange young man who did not appear to be motivated by sexuality. Even the report of Edgar Rice Burroughs had alluded to this fact.

During his examination, the doctor asked Hickman several pointed questions about his own sexuality. Hickman provided details, at the doctor's request, of his own sexual experiences with girls, which were limited. He discussed his first sexual emission and his rate of masturbation. Many women in court that day exhibited embarrassment. This was the 1920s, and despite the efforts of someone like Dr. Kinsey, such matters were not openly discussed.

Skoog's questions were important to the case, and Hickman's answers needed to be presented in court. No matter what terrible things had happened to Marion, it was made quite clear that nothing of a sexual nature had occurred. For that much, the nation could breathe a sigh of relief.

Throughout the testimony, Hickman sat stoic, his head down, and listened to Skoog relating their intimate conversation. The jury hung on every word, absorbing the information. The trial had been going on for days, and they would soon be called on to decide Hickman's fate.

Edward Hickman was not a patient man. He had resigned himself to hanging for the murder of Marion Parker and often told his attorneys that he simply wanted it over with. Walsh and Cantillon felt that their case was going well. They believed that their client would escape the gallows and serve a life sentence in an institution where his obvious lack of sanity would be monitored and his isolation would protect others. On several occasions, they reminded Hickman that his life was on the line, and they believed that they could save him from the gallows. Hickman would then calm down and realize that he was in good hands.

The nation exhibited impatience as well. As the trial was covered in newspapers across the country, the public anxiously awaited its outcome. Throughout the country, in virtually every city in every state, people were writing letters to their newspaper demanding that they wrap things up in California and "give this monster the execution he deserves."

The public cared nothing about his alleged insanity. Edward Hickman was a monster who killed and dismembered an innocent little girl. Marion Parker became the symbol of every child in America who could possibly be victim to the same kind of danger. Parents held their children a little closer, watched them a little more closely, and emphasized their rules in regard to any stranger who may approach them for whatever reason. Attendance in schools dropped sharply for a time. Parents were fearful. They seemed to feel that Hickman's being executed would send a message to potential child killers that such a practice would not always allow for the perpetrator to get away with an insanity defense, as Leopold and Loeb had.

While his defense attorneys were working hard to save him from the gallows, as Clarence Darrow had done for Leopold and Loeb, in the eyes of the public, Edward Hickman was a cold-blooded child killer who deserved to be hanged.

Juries are culled from the public.

CHAPTER 26

Jerry Walsh and Robert Cantillon felt that their case would likely be tried more by public sentiment than by the trial in which they were currently involved. The time had come for closing statements, and both of Hickman's attorneys felt that it was necessary that the defense open and close the arguments. They felt that because they carried the burden of proof, they should be the last side to be heard. The judge, however, disagreed.

Walsh and Cantillon realized what they were up against. They had defended a man who killed and dismembered an innocent twelve-year-old girl. The public had thirsted for the killer's blood since first reading of Marion Parker's ordeal in the newspapers. Now the first and last words were in the hands of the prosecution.

Shortly after court reconvened, Judge Trabucco asked Mr. Murray of the prosecuting team to make his summation.[1]

"Gentlemen of the defense, and ladies and gentlemen of the jury. This has been a long, arduous trial surcharged with disturbing emotion. It is nearly over. Very soon you jurors who attentively listened to the evidence will retire to deliberate upon a verdict. There is but a single issue of fact to be determined by you. It is this: did the defendant appreciate the character of his act and know it was wrong? That is the legal standard of responsibility. You dare not presume yourself wiser than the law. Judge Trabucco will charge you that if William Edward Hickman knew right from wrong in relation to the killing of Marion Parker, your verdict shall be that the defendant is sane.

"During the trial I have made judicious observation which I trust will be of assistance to you in reaching your decision that the defendant did know right from wrong. On July 15, 1927, in this identical courtroom, the same defendant stood before the court accused of forgery. The perpetrator of the crime had for his purpose the taking of another's money through fraud. Deliberate scheming and specific criminal intent accomplish forgery. The defendant, when caught, pleaded guilty, thus admitting that he knew the wrongfulness of that criminal act.

"Five months later the defendant is before this court accused of a kidnapping-murder. The perpetrator of his crime had for his purpose the taking of another's money through extortion. The crime here was also accomplished by deliberate scheming and specific criminal intent. The defendant, caught red-handed, pleads 'not guilty by reason of insanity,' thus asserting that he did not know the wrongfulness of that murderous act.

"Ladies and gentlemen, it is the difference in punishment for the crimes of forgery and murder that prompted the plea of 'not guilty by reason of insanity'; it is not a difference in the defendant's mental condition in July and December.

"Their defense of insanity rests on the premise that the defendant was under a delusion that he was directed and protected by a supernatural power in his killing of Marion Parker and did not know right from wrong. They illogically claim that the atrociousness of the crime proves this. I ask you to apply the touchstone of reason to the evidence to determine whether this premise is true or false. Always keep in mind that a man's knowledge of right from wrong can best be interpreted by his actions.

"Why did Hickman assume false names—the name Evans when he rented an apartment upon his arrival here from Kansas City; the name Cooper when he abducted the child from school; the name Palmer at a San Francisco hotel when in flight from California; the name Peck when the Pendleton police arrested him? He did this to avoid detention. Why? Because he knew he was guilty of premeditated kidnapping and murder and feared the consequences.

"Why did he repeatedly warn Mr. Parker in letters and telephone calls not to contact the police? It was because he knew he was guilty of a capital crime and, if apprehended, would be punished accordingly.

"When Hickman exchanged the mutilated remains of the child with her father for the gold certificates, why did he carry an automatic, bend his license plates, and mask his face? It transcends all reason to say he did not know full well the criminality of that grisly transaction.

"Why did Hickman abandon his Chrysler in which he delivered the child's body; at gun's point take a Hudson from its owner; and then flee the state of California? There is but one reason for such actions: his consciousness of guilt compelled him to become a fugitive from the justice he knew he deserved.

"All the matters embodied in these four questions conclusively imply the defendant's knowledge of the wrongfulness of his acts. For you jurors to find otherwise would be not only a fallacy, but folly. Ladies and gentlemen, you are the triers of fact. The sole issue for your considerations was whether or not Hickman knew his killing of Marion Parker was wrong. If he did, he is responsible to the law. There is but one verdict the evidence can support: the defendant is sane. His acts were the cruel, premeditated, deliberate acts of the calloused criminal. His was not the confused, purposeless act of the mentally sick. He committed this terrible crime to satisfy his greed for money. Hickman did not rely on a special Providence to protect him as he here represents. He relied upon criminal cunning and a fast shooting automatic pistol. He vowed he would kill his own poor mother, who struggled all her life to help him, if she interfered with his schemes.

"To me the defense of the insanity is a sham. It is as ridiculous as if the defendant had pleaded self defense. The bucket just doesn't hold water. I turn this case over to you. You have a most solemn duty to perform. You must not fail."

When reading these words in print, we are without the oral presentation that made the statement so much more powerful. Mr. Murray's eloquence and passionate delivery enhanced every word in the courtroom. The jury and the spectators sat quietly and pensively, drinking in all that Murray presented. His statement was clear and reasoned and had been beautifully delivered. Even Richard Cantillon would later write of Murray's eloquent presentation, the power of his speech, and how his inflections on each word enhanced their significance. He realized that such an act would be difficult to follow.

Murray had carefully presented the holes in the defense's argument, giving specific examples to back up his claim that Hickman was sane and in charge of his faculties and realized exactly what he was doing when he killed and dismembered Marion Parker. His indication of proof was compelling, and it subtly played to the sentiments of the public, who wanted Hickman to die for his offenses.

Walsh and Cantillon were listening as carefully as the jurors were. They had their statement for the defense prepared and would now augment their arguments against Murray's comments. They took careful notes, paying heed to those comments in Murray's statement that they could challenge effectively.

The judge called a ten-minute recess, after which it would be Walsh's turn to speak. Meanwhile, the jury discussed the prosecution's presentation.

Walsh and Cantillon huddled with their notes and discussed how they would use these within the context of their prepared statement. They were busy the entire ten minutes. Walsh and Cantillon had carefully gathered all of the points presented in the trial that helped prove their case that their client was insane. They also went over several points in the prosecution's speech that they felt could be effectively challenged with their statements. Walsh would be speaking first. Cantillon would follow him. Then the prosecution would get the final word. After that, the jury would deliberate for a verdict.

Meanwhile, these minutes ticked away much more slowly for Hickman. While he stated that he was resigned to being hanged for his crime, he did not appear to be completely absorbing the enormity of such a decision. He sat passively, his head down, offering no real connection to anyone else in the room other than the judge and his defense attorneys. Hickman was simply allowing things to happen and was prepared to respond to them once the final verdict was in. He did not express any real fear or any genuine remorse. He merely cooperated. He did not engage in outlandish behavior in order to help "sell" an insanity defense as presented by his defense team.

Ten minutes elapsed, and Walsh and Cantillon were ready.

CHAPTER 27

As the ten-minute recess ended, everyone returned to court. Defense attorney Jerome Walsh, exuding the confidence of someone prepared and in control, approached the bench.[1]

"May I now proceed, your Honor?"

"Proceed, Mr. Walsh."

"The Prosecutor, Murray, has selected a little pile of triviality from the mass of weighty evidence, and by inlaying these small pieces of various colored circumstances, he has fabricated a mosaic with which he hopes to dazzle your judgment. These special circumstances can be summed up as the defendant's concealment of his identity, his avoidance of detection, the use of deadly weapons, and the flight from this state. Murray has taken these incidents out of context to prove William Edward Hickman sane. When we properly consider Murray's incidents along with the major acts preceding and following, they are but tints on the powerful portrait of schizophrenia.

"If you carefully consider my worthy opponent's argument, you will find that it is composed of three propositions. First, that the defendant's fear of consequences proves that he knew right from wrong in relation to the act of killing. Second, that greed for money motivated the defendant to kill Marion Parker. Third, that you should accept as true the opinions given by medical witnesses produced by the prosecutors. If you will, as Mr. Murray requested, and here I insist, apply the touchstone of reason, I am certain that the evidence to which I will draw your attention will contradict each and all of the prosecutions contentions.

"We will consider the first proposition that the defendant feared the consequences of his act. If the preponderance of the evidence establishes that the defendant could not entertain a fear of consequence, this theory contended for by the prosecutor is refuted. What is fear? It is a strong emotion caused by an awareness of danger.

"On the subject of fear, the evidence establishes that the defendant repeatedly precipitated situations fraught with danger. Can he be said to have feared the danger he deliberately created? When the defendant openly kidnapped Marion Parker from a public school, he toyed with danger. He courted danger on Friday night when, with the kidnapped child in his automobile, he rode in the police procession to Tenth and Gramercy. He defied danger and death when he delivered the child's mutilated body to her father, whom he had every reason to believe would be accompanied by the police. He exhibited absolute disregard for danger when, knowing an intensive police search for him was in full swing, he went to the busy intersection of Western and Hollywood and robbed Fred Peck of his automobile.

"The insanity of this boy is made manifest by his inability to react normally to the awareness of danger. His emotional functioning which produces fear is peculiarly paralyzed by schizophrenia, a dread disease.

"Warnings, weapons, concealment of identity, and flight are all in the nature of innate impulses and are circumstances far subordinate to the major facts of this case. These incidents do not establish the sanity of one who strangled a child, mutilated her body, wired open the eyes, and rouged the face, and delivered it to her father for $1,500. Particularly is this so when it develops that his money is wanted for a religious education. The major facts as proof of insanity far outweigh the minor circumstances on which Mr. Murray predicates his sanity claim. Your findings on this issue in this case must be made on the overall picture, not just isolated incidents as Mr. Murray urges.

"Mr. Murray further asserts that the defendant was motivated to kill Marion Parker by his greed for money. Apparently the prosecution and the defense are not too far apart in their respective appraisals of this case. Greed is a desire for money that exceeds the limit of reason. As counsel for the defendant, I too agree that the defendant's inordinate money acquisitiveness exceeded the limit of reason. Yes! It exceeded the limit of rationality. It spawns directly from his insane delusion; it is stark madness. In the Kansas City depositions, prosecutor Costello asked Mr. Laughlin, the Assistant High School Principal, if it would change his opinion that Hickman was insane if he knew his motive for killing Marion Parker was to obtain $1,500 to defray his expenses at Park College. Mr. Laughlin logically analyzed the defendant's morbid self-contradictory behavior. Hickman's purpose was to become an Evangelist and reconcile sinful man to God through Christ, so in furtherance of this purpose, he had killed God's greatest treasure, a guileless little girl. 'No, Mr. Costello,' Laughlin replied, 'it would not change my opinion; it would make me feel more than ever that the boy is insane because Park College is an ecclesiastical institution.'

"Mr. Murray on the proposition of greed tells but half of the story. The defendant was indeed possessed of a desire for $1,500 that exceeded the limits of reason. But Mr. Murray doesn't tell you that this obsessive desire stemmed from an insane delusion that Almighty Providence directed the defendant to acquire this money for schooling to become a minister of Christ. This is the whole story. On the greed issue the facts in their entirety preponderated in favor of the defense.

"Each of you jurors took a sacred oath that you could and would eradicate bias and prejudice from your thinking and return a verdict based solely upon the evidence in this case. The evidence overwhelmingly establishes that this boy suffers from mental disease. It clearly shows that he conjured, through sick fantasy, a false God. His disease-twisted thinking affected transference of the obedience due the Almighty to his morbid Providence. At this Providence's command, he killed Marion Parker. In this fevered mental state, he could not know right from wrong.

"'Thou Shalt Not Kill' is an admonition not alone from the sovereign state, but from Almighty God. It applies with equal force to all competent, responsible mortals. This may be the only time in your lives when you come face to face with this divine injunction. If one of you sitting in the jury box should in the deliberations join in a verdict adverse to this boy, motivated by prejudice or to gain public approbation, you will have violated the commandment of God, 'Thou shalt not kill.' And that one will be called upon to pay the awful penalty for perfidy and murder in God's chosen manner, in God's chosen time."

Walsh slowly returned to his seat at the counsel table. During his statement, he paused and slowly drank a glass of water, adding further dramatic effect. He basically stated that the jurors would be murderers in the same vein as Hickman, as far as the judgment of God is concerned, if they put this mentally unstable man to death. It was an interesting defense argument, weighing on the morals and superstitions of the jurors.

It was also clever of Walsh to indicate that Hickman's lack of fear or nervousness in perpetrating this very serious crime alludes also to his lack of sanity. The jurors could see this demonstrated as Walsh spoke. Hickman was on trial for his very life and sat quietly with his head down, expressing no real emotion at all. Walsh points out that Hickman was unaware of the danger he was in with the kidnapping and eventual murder. And the jury could clearly see Hickman in the courtroom, expressing no sense of danger while his right to keep living was on trial.

On Walsh's conclusion, the court declared a two-hour adjournment for lunch. It would be Richard Cantillon's turn to speak for the defense when court reconvened. Cantillon skipped lunch and spent the two hours in the law library to concentrate on his presentation. After Cantillon concluded with his presentation, District Attorney Keyes would have the final word for the prosecution. Because the prosecution would be following him with the last word, Cantillon realized that his address to the jury had to be even more forceful than Walsh's had been.

CHAPTER 28

Richard Cantillon was back in court at 2:00 p.m. and given the judge's direction to proceed. He had spent a great deal of time preparing his statement, realizing that it would be the last the jury would hear from the defense. He knew that his spot was an important one. He would be offering the final words regarding the insanity defense of his client, William Edward Hickman. It was not, however, the last statement to be presented in court. The prosecution would have the last word. Cantillon had to convince the jury completely as to the insanity of his client. His words would have to be so powerful that they could not be refuted or overshadowed by the subsequent final word from the prosecution. No details could be overlooked.

The defense attorney thanked the court and jury and paid his respects to the prosecution. He then began his statement, which would conclude the final words of the defense for the jury to ponder. [1]

"When you were questioned at the time you were first called into the jury box, all of you stated that you entertained a preconceived opinion. I am not insensible to the nature of that opinion. The panic and terror of that awful Saturday night incensed revulsion and revenge. Each of you swore that you would banish from you mind your preconceived opinion and base your verdict solely on the evidence. It was upon this solemn assurance that you qualified to act as a trier of the fact in the case at bar. As sworn jurors, you became a component of the judiciary. No longer can you entertain beliefs of sanity or insanity upon rumor and report. Your decision must be based only upon judicial evidence. That is, the sworn testimony given by the witnesses, the sworn testimony read from the depositions, and the exhibits introduced during the trial. To consider rumor or report secretly or openly in your deliberations would be to violate your sacred oath.

"As trial jurors, it is your duty to accept and apply the law as given to you by the trial judge. The Court will charge you that under law an insane man is incapable of committing murder or any other crime. This is a cardinal principle of criminal justice. You as jurors dare not presume yourselves wiser than the law. The question as to whether William Edward Hickman is sane or insane is not one of medical science or legal definition. It is a question to be answered by your common sense. An impartial consideration of the evidence will satisfy you that it is far more probable the boy is insane.

"We must consider the nature of insanity. It is a disorder of the thought processes of the mind. The mind is capable of definition only as it relates to its functions. It thinks, it feels, it wills, and thereby governs all human behavior. The psychiatrists call these functions intellection, emotion, and volition. The brain, the organ of the mind, is a mass of nerve tissue contained within the cranium. The special function of this organ has been said, by analogy, to secrete thought as the liver secretes bile. The brain is subject to the ravages of disease as are the lungs, the heart, and all other bodily organs. When this occurs, the interconnected mental functions become deranged and the thoughts fantastic, resulting in bizarre behavior that is often dangerous.

"Our defense is that William Edward Hickman is sick, desperately sick. He suffers from a mental disease called schizophrenia. The doctors for the prosecution and the defense agree that the predisposing cause of schizophrenia is heredity. They agree that an unstable environment and puberty are the precipitating factors; that a personality change and fixed, systematized, dominant delusion accompanies the disease. Here all agreement among these professional men ends. The doctors for the defense claim this boy is pathetically insane, and that all essential symptoms for a diagnosis of schizophrenia are present. The doctors for the prosecution say that he is sane and his behavior normal. They cannot find in all his frightful evidence a single symptom of mental derangement. Between this conflicting evidence it is your duty to exercise common sense and determine wherein the truth lies.

"To aid you in your deliberations, it is my purpose to focus your attention on evidence which clearly proves, to the point of demonstration, that the defendant is insane. On the subject of the defendant's heredity and environment during his formative years, sixteen witnesses from the Ozarks testified. They were the immediate family, relatives, neighbors, attending physicians, and a registered nurse. The prosecution produced nothing contradictory, although it commands the financial and legal resources of the State of California and has the cooperation of authorities everywhere.

"The witnesses painted a picture of an old woman tortured by paranoid delusions—Becky Buck, the crazy grandmother of the defendant.

"Witnesses also described a Bible-reading old man, a religious camp meeting revivalist who, when triggered by the slightest incident, would fly into rages—Paul Buck, the psycho-neurotic grandfather of the defendant.

"Graphically these witnesses then etched a poor 'slobbering, wallowing' epileptic imbecile, who foolishly followed his wife while she worked in the fields for their subsistence. This was Otto Buck, the defendant's first cousin.

"These witnesses further drew a word picture of a mother standing in a dim light over her sleeping children, butcher knife upraised; a wife silently moving in night-darkened hallways, hatchet in hand, bent on killing her husband; a woman frustrated in her homicidal efforts drinking a caustic acid in an attempt at self destruction; a woman committed to the state asylum as dangerously insane. This was Eva Hickman, the schizophrenic mother of the defendant.

"Interwoven in this proof of insane heredity is the evidence of the precipitating factor of an unstable environment. The nocturnal screams and struggles, his demented mother's attempts at homicide and suicide, the frenzied religious exorcisms to which the grandfather subjected the child, sudden desertion by this father, the obsessive hate, privation, and hunger were the soil where the seed flourished.

"The power of procreation in the male begins at puberty. He is then between twelve to fourteen years of age. Puberty is accompanied by drastic bodily changes which continue into the maturity of his twenties. To a boy predisposed to schizophrenia, this is a critical period, as schizophrenia is the disease of adolescence. Medical experts are becoming convinced from their research that it is the alteration in the chemistry of the body, brought on by the glandular changes that results in the pubescent shock, which is so devastating to the adolescent, predisposed to schizophrenia.

"The facts of this case amply establish the drastic change in the personality of William Edward Hickman which accompanied his pubescent bodily changes. The doctors consider this change an essential symptom of schizophrenia. Through witnesses who knew him best in his high school days, fellow students, teachers, adult friends, and employers, we showed that this boy possessed all the sterling qualities that we look for in an outstanding man.

"With great courage he overcame the almost insurmountable obstacles that poverty places in the path of the poor. Although compelled to work for a living, his intellectual attainments surpassed those of any of the 3,000 students in Central High School. He participated in all oratorical contests, winning or placing highly in these endeavors. His fellow students elected him Vice President of their senior class. He became President of the school chapter of the National Honor Society. He was deeply religious; his goal was the ministry. He was sensitive to suffering, sacrificing his limited recreation time to visit a friend who was in his last illness. This tenderhearted boy could not bring himself to kill a chicken.

"Within a period of months, we find him in this courtroom on trial for murder. What caused the terrible change in this boy's personality? The answer is disease. You have seen a strong body rendered helplessly crippled by polio. Here you see a strong mind rendered hopelessly maniacal by schizophrenia.

"Now let me take up the matter of the defendant's delusion. This is, by its very nature, the difficult symptom to prove because it is subjective; that is, perceptible only to the deranged one. The defendant, in his written statement made for District Attorney Keyes en route from Oregon to Los Angeles, referred to this delusion. I will read a portion of that writing from the exhibit in evidence.

"'The fact that I, a young man, was willing to commit murder to secure expenses through college, and especially a church school, helps to explain me. This was my great motive. I cannot understand it myself. In the murder of Marion Parker, I could not realize this terrible guilt. I felt Providence was guiding and directing me in this.'

"District Attorney Keyes signed this written statement as a witness. I cannot say what Mr. Keyes's reaction was to the defendant's reference to his Providence. But this I know; the District Attorney had a brain surgeon, Dr. C., waiting for Hickman's arrival at the county jail. Why? In the jury room in your deliberations, you jurors ask and answer that question.

"In every psychiatric examination of the boy thereafter, he repeated his relationship to this strange Deity he called Providence. Did he believe this? The matters I will call to your attention will convince you that he did. Religion is recognition on the part of man of a controlling Superhuman Power entitled to obedience. The dominant influence in this boy's childhood was his grandfather, Paul Buck, who followed the Biblical proverb, 'Train up the child in the way he should go and when he is old he will not depart from it.' In his zealotry, the grandfather exposed his grandchild to frenzied religious exorcisms, placing further strain on this child's predisposed emotional instability.

"When mental disease distorted the boy's thinking processes, he became incapable of attaining his life's goal. He withdrew into a world of sick imagination. Here his burning ambition was more than satisfied; he became the sole earthly agent of a Super God and the only object of his bounty. In return he permuted the absolute obedience due his Maker to this false Super God. Out of limbo of his subconscious mind, surcharged with severe repressions of his awful childhood, homicide and mutilation ideated. These repressions stemmed from the conduct and threats of his demented mother, as testified by his father. When his Super God commanded him to take a human life, this boy was powerless to disobey. Under such delusive influence, he strangled Marion Parker.

"When Hickman hung that little dead body head down over the bathtub drain and cut the throat with a kitchen knife, when he severed the arms and legs, when he disemboweled the child, when he dressed what remained of her in her school clothes, when he rouged her face, applied lipstick to that little dead mouth, and wired open the eyes, he was not malingering—he was completely mad.

"Under the enlightened influence of civilization a refined law decrees the non-responsibility of one suffering from insanity. This is the charity of the law. Regardless of public excitement and vindictiveness, this is the law of our land and upon the strength and courage of your jurors, its just application rests. These all are the bizarre acts of a diseased mind. They have caused horror and loathing, but it is this boy's mental condition upon which your verdict must be grounded, not on your emotional reaction to his irrational behavior."

With that, Richard Cantillon concluded his statement. He and Walsh had spoken. Hickman's defense team had done everything they could for their client. The jurors listened carefully to both of them.

Years later, when writing a book about this case,[2] Richard Cantillon recalled being pleased with his presentation for the defense. Indeed, it was an excellent argument in favor of his client. He had broken down the defense presented during the trial, discussing again Hickman's history and his choices. The line "You have seen a strong body rendered helplessly crippled by polio. Here you see a strong mind rendered hopelessly maniacal by schizophrenia" was a good example that jurors could understand. Polio did attack someone quite suddenly, and then it would gradually deplete a person's body. Cantillon wanted to make the comparison to how a mind might plummet in power the same way as would a body. Hickman, he argued, was a victim of his own mind.

Cantillon had matched the eloquence of his predecessors and made it difficult for the subsequent final word from the prosecution to argue against his points. But William Edward Hickman murdered and dismembered an innocent little girl. That was still the reason anyone was in that courtroom, including the jury assigned to decide the killer's fate.

CHAPTER 29

It was now time to conclude the entire trial with the statement from District Attorney Asa Keyes. He had been a part of the case since the beginning and had ridden on a train from Oregon to California with Hickman. He had been witness to Hickman's initial confessions and had heard the conversation that was not a part of those confessions: the conversation that "Hard-Boiled" Herman Cline alluded to when he stated that the gruesome facts of the case would hang Hickman.

The gruesome facts of the case were not out. Journalism was such that the most graphic descriptions would not be allowed in the mainstream press. The public knew the gist of the murder but not all of the gory details. But the jury had heard everything. It was they who would decide Hickman's fate.

In defense of their client, both Richard Cantillon and Jerome Walsh argued that this horrible act was the result of a sick mind. It was the jury's job to decide whether Hickman was indeed insane at the time he committed the murder or whether he was acting out of pure evil stemming from greed and malice.

But first, they had to hear from the district attorney, and Asa Keyes was a clever man who possessed a sardonic wit that he injected into his statements to add color and verve. It was always effective, especially when dealing with the prejudices of a jury against a child killer like Hickman.

Stepping out into the center of the court, addressing the jury, Keyes delivered the statement that he hoped would effectively conclude this trial with the ruling that Hickman was not insane.[1]

"These young men who have undertaken the defense of this defendant have done a masterful job," Keyes began.

"I am pleased.

"No one witnessing this trial can ever say the defendant has not had the full measure of his rights. This establishes confidence and respect for our judicial system. For if people did not have confidence and respect for the jury system and know that justice will be done, Hickman would not be here today. If people were not civilized, the mob would take this man from the law officers. I would have been in the forefront of a mob trying to put a noose around the neck of the defendant if I did not honor the law.

"I'm not going to get into the horrible details of this crime. We have been criticized for giving this man a trial at all by certain people."

On hearing this statement, both Cantillon and Walsh exploded into loud objections from their seats at the defense table. It was deemed prejudicial by the judge, and the jurors were asked not to consider Mr. Keyes's remarks as evidence.

But Keyes knew that the jury had already heard him.

"I'm going to be fair to Hickman," Keyes continued, "although I loathe the ground he walks on.

"Do you know that it is the duty of the D.A. prosecuting the defendant to guard his rights and see that no right is violated? It is not the duty of the D.A. to inflame the jury's mind against the defendant.

"Hickman started his insanity dodge in the Pendleton jail and he's just as smart now as when he won second place in the oratorical contest in Kansas City. He knew the only way to attempt to dodge the gallows was by insanity, and he was smart enough to try to fool the jury. Dr. Skoog submitted the defendant to asinine tests that I never heard of before.

"Do you think this man who committed this crime when he took the body to the father and grabbed the $1,500, armed with a loaded gun, believed he was directed by Divine Providence to give a great message to the world? He did not tell the father, 'I committed this crime so the eyes of the world would be directed to me.' He acted like every other criminal. At the point of a gun, he took the $1,500 and drove away in his stolen automobile, and made the detection impossible. He did not say, 'I want the eyes of the world upon me for the commission of this crime.' He did not want the eyes of the world upon him; he sought to cover so not a single eye on the face of the earth could see him. Old Doc Skoog, the country gentleman from Kansas City, swallowed what Hickman told him hook, line, and sinker.

"Most of the crimes committed in the United States are committed by young men between the ages of fifteen and twenty-three. Whether a young man goes straight or crooked is not shaped by Divine Providence, but by himself. Hickman is not insane; he is bad, rotten to the core. He committed grave crimes after he left high school and the parental roof. He did not want to apply himself to work; he wanted to make money the easy way.

"Don't you see, ladies and gentlemen of the jury, don't you gather from what these doctors tell you about this demential praecox, paranoid form, that a man who is really afflicted with that, that a man who really has it, that a man who really commits a crime guided and influenced and directed by his insane delusion tells you all? He is proud of it; his mind is full of it; he can't think of anything else. You know that is a fact. They tell you so. That has been their observation; that has been my observation. Don't you believe that if this defendant had really and truly had, at the time or has now, dementia praecox of the paranoid type, that when he was arrested there in Pendleton, and old man Gurdane, the gentleman who covered him with a gun and put him under arrest, first talked to him, what would have been the most natural thing for that man to have uttered when is asked his name? They say he is full of grandiose ideas, exalted ego. He said his name was Peck. Was there any exalted ego in that statement? Was there anything in those actions to lead you to believe that he was actuated or had any grandiose ideas?

"A sane man would do just exactly as the Fox did on that occasion. If he had been insane, ladies and gentlemen, if he had dementia praecox, paranoid form, with the delusion which these doctors say he had, he would have said, 'Mr. Chief of Police, my name is William Edward Hickman. I killed the Parker girl, but I did it because I was guided by a divine providence. I did it because I want my name to be blazoned across the portals of mankind down through the ages, to go as the perpetrator of the most atrocious crime that has ever been committed in the United States. I am proud of it. I have been directed by divine providence, by my Supreme Being, to do it.' He did not say that, did he? No, he did not, and he never mentioned anything about a divine providence to any single living soul, or never claimed that he was guided by it until he had time to figure out in the Pendleton jail what his defense in this matter was going to be.

"I think he was a monster without a soul, without conscience, without a heart. When he committed forgery, he made no claim that divine providence had guided him. He printed his ransom notes to disguise his handwriting so his identity would be kept in the dark. If he thought he was guided by Providence, why would he be trying to conceal his identity? Hickman did not believe in God. He who believes he is above the Savior of mankind penned a note to the poor suffering father informing him to ask God for aid.

"A lot of people say they can't understand how Hickman could have committed such a crime if he was in his right mind. He is a criminal; he is a bad man; he is a man without a soul, without a conscience, without a heart. He is not an All-American boy; he is an American criminal who, with the aid of your verdict, the State of California will purge from its borders. I want the jury to show the people of the United States what the far western state of California says to people who commit crimes like this within its borders.

"There have been mobs formed in the city of Los Angeles to deal with this man. All the way from Pendleton until we got to Los Angeles, there were mobs at every station. I've stood behind this boy to see that no mob violence overtook him; he's entitled to that. If it were to come to pass through any effort of mine that the law of the State of California was to become a mockery, it would be better for me if I had never been born.

"I'm going to submit this matter to you at this time with the hope that it does not go out to the Atlantic seaboard and the countries of the world that the state of California is not able to adequately cope with a criminal, because a criminal the man is; he is not insane."

With that, Keyes concluded his statement, and the trial for William Edward Hickman, killer of Marion Parker, was over. After more than a month of screaming headlines in newspapers throughout the nation, keeping the public informed of every step of the kidnapping, ransom, murder, pursuit of the criminal, and eventual capture, the trial completed in a mere fifteen days. It was now time for the jury to decide his fate. The jury was not to decide Hickman guilty or innocent of killing Marion Parker. Hickman had confessed to the murder. But was he guilty or not guilty by reason of insanity? "It is not every kind or degree of insanity which renders a person incapable of committing crime," Judge Trabucco told the court.[2]

Addressing the jury, the judge defined insanity as "such a diseased and deranged condition of the mental faculties as to render the person incapable of knowing the nature and quality of the act or of distinguishing between right and wrong in relation to the act with which he is charged.

"You are to determine what the condition of the defendant's mind as at the precise time of the commission of the acts charged in the indictment. Its condition before or afterward is only to be considered by you for the purpose of throwing light upon its state of the commission of said acts."

The jury retired to decide Hickman's fate at 2:20 p.m. In forty-three minutes, they were back in court, ready to deliver their verdict. It had taken less than an hour for the twelve men and women to determine what should be done with William Edward Hickman.

CHAPTER 30

When the jury returned to the courtroom after forty-three minutes of deliberation, the verdict was presented. The vote was unanimous. Hickman was sane. He did know what he was doing when he murdered and dismembered Marion Parker. He did understand right from wrong. He was able to comprehend the extent of his actions. He was legally responsible for his crimes.

Hickman sat quietly with little expression as the verdict was read. The prosecution shook hands. The defense held their heads. And the courtroom erupted into noisy applause as the judge pounded his gavel.

It has become a cliché of movies regarding trials to have reporters rush out of a courtroom and get to a telephone to relay important news to the editorial desk at their respective papers. Long before the advent of cellular phones, these journalists would hurry to special telephone outlets set up for their use. Virtually anyone who has seen an old courtroom drama can recall a scene where reporters would run to a row of telephones, hollering the verdict into the mouthpiece. It wasn't Hollywood's penchant for creating drama. This is exactly how it happened when the verdict for William Edward Hickman was read in court.

The next day, newspapers across the nation triumphantly announced that Hickman was declared sane. He was responsible for the killing and dismembering of little Marion Parker. The case that District Attorney Keyes referred to as "the most atrocious crime ever committed in the United States" and that had become a part of pop culture by finding its way into newspaper editorial cartoons, poems, and the repertoire of folksingers had concluded with this verdict.

Essays in editorial columns speculated Hickman's fate. Death by hanging was the standard in California at that time, held over from the western frontier days that, in 1927, did not lie too distantly in the past. Would Hickman be hanged? Would he be sentenced to life in prison? The public eagerly read accounts in various newspaper editorials and discussed it among themselves. Citizens in every city in every state throughout the nation had been talking about the case as it unfolded. Everyone, it appeared, had an opinion. The general consensus was that Hickman should hang. His guilty verdict was celebrated by some, with reports of parties being thrown in honor of Marion Parker and condemning Hickman as a convicted killer who would now meet a much-deserved end.

An emotionally exhausted Perry Parker spoke only briefly to the press. He indicated that he was glad the trial was over and that the jury realized it was his little girl, not Hickman, who was the victim in this case. Parker stated that he and his family simply wanted to get on with their lives. It was something that he would continue to say to the press until the case faded from the headlines and the newspapers finally left the Parker family alone to actually get on with their lives.

William Edward Hickman had sat quietly in the courtroom and listened to his family history and various quirks paraded before the courts. The facts, the various testimonies, and the statements by prosecutors and defense attorneys were examined by a jury of his peers. Everything was subsequently reported in the press. Hickman heard testimony from family, friends, doctors, and law officials. They all saw through his ruse—he was sane, and they knew it. So did he. Hickman had earlier stated that he knew he would "swing" and still exhibited the same detached calmness after the verdict was read.

While the prosecutors declared victory, Hickman's defense team was shocked by the verdict. They could not fathom how Hickman, with his family history and the horrible crime he committed, had been determined to be sane, to be in full charge of his mental faculties. They started putting together a possible appeal, some logical way to change Judge Trabucco's decision.

The judge scheduled sentencing for the following Saturday.

CHAPTER 31

On Saturday, February 11, 1928, William Edward Hickman was back in court with his defense team of Jerome Walsh and Richard Cantillon, to be given his sentence by Judge Trabucco. Meanwhile, back in Ada, Oklahoma, the mayor and the PTA sought an injunction to bar any newsreel footage featuring Hickman to play in the town's movie houses. The ban was made official that same Saturday. Hickman's photographic image was deemed too offensive for the Ada cinemas, where people went to relax and enjoy the movies. William Edward Hickman represented such a level of evil that his photographic image was banned from an entire city.

But in court, it was Jerome Walsh who issued a challenge. He and Cantillon had worked hard for the past several days in a continued, rather desperate attempt to save their client from the hangman's noose. Walsh and Cantillon appeared in court with a four-page list of twenty specifically detailed reasons arguing for Hickman's sentence to be deferred. Walsh's aim was to get Hickman a new trial, which would buy all of them the much-needed time to increase their insanity defense.

Along with Richard Cantillon's assistance, Walsh challenged Judge Trabucco's presentation, the opinion of the jurors, defense objections that he felt were unfairly denied, that some of the written testimonies read in court violated Hickman's Fifth Amendment rights, and so on. Walsh also claimed that the defense had new evidence that had been gathered since court adjourned after the jury's verdict.

Judge Trabucco was overwhelmed by the defense's claims and the details of their challenge. It was too much to examine and make a determination immediately. So Judge Trabucco adjourned court until Tuesday morning, February 14, Valentine's Day. When that day arrived, everyone was back in court to hear Walsh submit the following: [1]

A motion in arrest of judgment

A formal submission of the new-trial motion

A nine-point list of objections that took issue with the court's jurisdiction

Both motions were denied, and the objections were overruled. After all the work that the defense attorneys had done to get some extra time, stall the process, and perhaps obtain a new trial, their attempts failed. The prosecution delivered two familiar witnesses. Dr. A. F. Wagner once again described the condition of Marion Parker's body on his examination on December 17 and 18 and presented the gruesome morgue photos that had been introduced during the trial. He again indicated that he was a neighbor of the Parker family and that working on Marion's body was among the most difficult postmortem examinations that he ever had to perform.

Chief Herman Cline was obviously perturbed at having to offer evidence regarding William Edward Hickman's fiendishness again after he was found guilty by a jury and about to be sentenced by the presiding judge. Herman Cline exhibited a real impatience with the judicial process and merely presented a truncated account of the manhunt for Marion's killer. Giving only the highlights and few of the noted details, Cline seasoned his presentation with excerpts of Hickman's confessions.

Walsh appeared desperate when he moved to have the testimony of both men stricken from the record. This motion was also denied. The judge now addressed the court, fully prepared with his sentence. [2]

"The court now determines and finds that the degree of crime in count two of the indictment is murder of the first degree without extenuating or mitigating circumstances."

Walsh and Cantillon sat in their chairs, defeated. The judge continued.

"William Edward Hickman, stand up."

Hickman stood and faced the judge. Looking directly into Judge Trabucco's eyes, Hickman was completely still, offering a stoicism that did not go unnoticed by the reporters in attendance.

"It is the judgment and sentence of this court, that for the crime of kidnapping, the offense described in count one of the indictment, that you, William Edward Hickman, be confined in the state prison of the state of California, at San Quentin, for the term prescribed by law, which term will be fixed by the Board of Prison directors.

"Testimony was received by the court for the purpose of ascertaining and determining the degree of the crime charged in count two of the indictment—to wit, murder. The court, after due consideration, determines and finds that the degree of the crime in count two of the indictment is murder of the first degree without extenuating and mitigating circumstances, and that for the crime of murder, the offense described in count two of the indictment, you shall suffer the penalty of death. Therefore, it is the judgment and sentence of this court, William Edward Hickman, that for the crime of which you have been convicted—to wit, murder in the first degree—that you be delivered by the sheriff of Los Angeles County to the warden of the state prison of the state of California at San Quentin, to be by him executed and put to death on Friday, the 27th day of April, 1928, in the manner provided by the state of California. And may God have mercy on your soul."

Of course, the swiftness of the sentencing would not be carried out as quickly as April 27, which was only two months away. Walsh and Cantillon were not giving up, and any appeals or other such circumstances would drag things out. Walsh, in fact, started immediately by moving that the death sentence be revoked on the grounds that Judge Trabucco was out of his legal jurisdiction. That motion was also denied.

But the defense was undaunted. They were not merely working for their client as a part of the judicial process; they also personally believed Hickman to be insane. Only a true madman could kill and dismember a little girl and then later claim that he loved her. They continued to repeat that insanity was proven by his family history, the volatile nature he had exhibited in the past, and his actions since being incarcerated. The jury might have submitted a verdict, and the judge may have sentenced their client, but Walsh and Cantillon were by no means finished working.

CHAPTER 32

While his lawyers attempted to investigate other ways of proving their tried and sentenced client insane, Hickman's own time in court had not ended. He still had the Ivy Thoms murder trial to endure. This time, he was not alone. His old friend and crime partner Welby Hunt accompanied him. Hunt continued to deny having fired his gun. Ballistics testing indicated, however, that a .38 killed Thoms, and it was Hunt himself who admitted to carrying that caliber of gun during the robbery when Thoms fell. His account checked out with Hickman's when each had been interviewed separately.

It appeared that the public at large deemed the trial for the Thoms murder comparatively anticlimactic. It did not become a focal point of the nation's press as had the Marion Parker trial. Hickman was already sentenced to death for the Marion Parker murder. He could die only once. The fate of Welby Hunt was not interesting to the public at large. Hunt never attacked a child; he merely committed a robbery and allegedly killed an innocent man during the holdup. He may have also been instrumental in the death of his own grandfather, but he was not a child killer. Welby Hunt was perceived as just another murderous punk who was about to be put away. This was not a high-profile case in the media. And, like the Parker trial, the Thoms trial was also wrapped up in a relatively quick manner. After sixteen days, both Hunt and Hickman were found equally guilty of Thoms's murder. And Hickman was once again declared sane.

Welby Hunt could not be hanged because he was only a minor at the time of the murder. He was therefore sentenced to life in prison. To the end of his days, Hunt expressed anger and hatred toward his former friend for turning him in and insisted that he was innocent in the Thoms murder. Hickman was no longer his partner in crime but rather a convicted child killer who had murdered druggist Ivy Thoms and allowed the blame to fall on the innocent Welby Hunt.

Hickman and Hunt were shackled together and brought to San Quentin Prison on March 17, 1928. They made the trip in silence. According to deputies, on arriving at the prison, Hickman stated that he, not Welby Hunt, had killed Thoms. There is some speculation as to why Hickman said this, at least one writer believing that perhaps he was trying to achieve some prison notoriety for this murder, realizing that child killers were likely ill-treated by prisoners. In any case, exactly why Hickman insisted that he killed Thoms, going against all previous statements and evidence, is not known.

Edward Hickman was registered at San Quentin as inmate number 45041. During his medical examination, Hickman joked with the physician, Dr. Stanley, while stripped down, asking him to look at his muscles as he flexed his comparatively small biceps. Hickman felt like talking. He seemed to want to talk about his murder more and more frequently now that he was indeed going to be executed for it. He talked to the doctor throughout the examination.

Hickman blamed Perry Parker for making the mistake of trusting him. He indicated that Parker should have telephoned the police the minute he knew Marion was kidnapped in spite of the note warning him not to because "no crook plays fair." Hickman called himself a master crook. "I felt no pity for the father. I felt no remorse at all. I just felt I was executing a master stroke. As for the little girl, she's better off than I am. At least she's out of this world of turmoil and strife. I no longer believe in a heaven or hell, but I know we shall have everlasting life.

"Any man has the right to hold up another man if he wants to. Even if the holdup results in murder, it is all right. Everything is foreordained. Our lives are mapped out for us from the beginning. What I have done was my destiny. I could not help it."[1]

As Hickman settled on San Quentin's death row, his defense attorneys were spending their days trying to find a way to appeal his conviction. Meanwhile, Hickman's captors, Buck Lieuallen and Tom Gurdane, were still hunting for their reward money. What had been initially tallied at around $90,000 had now been altered to around $50,000. Then another $10,000 was shaved off when the Los Angeles City Council ruled that it could not legally post rewards. Thereafter, various other donors backed out on their initial pledges. Finally, it was reported that only a few thousand dollars remained. Lieuallen and Gurdane returned home to Oregon, achieving little more than local status for capturing the most notorious fugitive America had known up to that time. They returned to their work and their lives and only occasionally discussed their joint capture of William Edward Hickman and the pittance of a reward that had dwindled from nearly $100,000 to only a few thousand. Lieuallen later stated that it seemed obvious that the authorities didn't want the money to leave California.

Hickman's verdict generated a tangible public reaction. There were letters to newspapers across the country, most of them applauding the decision. The public was sending letters to the judge, the attorneys, and officials at San Quentin. Many people had followed the trial closely in the newspapers, just as the O. J. Simpson trial would be followed closely nearly seventy years later. There was no television, so people relied on the press. Some took it personally. There was more than one request that Hickman be hanged on a specific date, namely, his birthday.

A gaggle of conspiracy theorists insisted that Hickman did not act alone, that he was railroaded, and that justice had not been served. Underground meetings were scheduled, and grassroots efforts were made to get Hickman another trial. Walsh and Cantillon had nothing to do with this movement, and law enforcement as well as the public generally ignored it. It received some marginal notoriety in the press but petered out rather quickly.

Of course, the continued appeals presented by the defense extended Hickman's life. As predicted, his sentenced execution date did not occur so swiftly as to happen in April. Hickman would be allowed to live through another spring and another summer—albeit from a prison cell on San Quentin's death row.

The press and the public were impatient. Letters from angry citizens continued to fill newspapers throughout the nation, wondering why it was taking so long "to put that monster away forever." The *Los Angeles Times* printed an editorial in August 1928 complaining how the Hickman situation had dragged on for so many months. It asked the question on the minds of many: Why was Hickman still languishing on death row? The public and the press wanted to know, and their escalating reaction pressured law enforcement officials.

Perhaps as a result of public outcry, perhaps due to editorials, or maybe because the defense had exhausted its efforts to save their client from the gallows, Warden James Holohan of San Quentin Prison was ordered to execute William Edward Hickman by hanging on October 19, 1928.

The American public started marking their calendars.

So did William Edward Hickman.

CHAPTER 33

William Edward Hickman spent the next several months preparing for his fate. He felt the need to write letters to the families of his victims and to law enforcement officials in the towns where he had committed crimes. Hickman considered this to be something of a spiritual cleansing: to make amends for what he considered his past mistakes and remove these crimes from his damaged soul. He told the press that these letters were part of his plan to get right with God.

He penned the following to the widow of the slain druggist, Ivy Thoms:[1]

> Dear friend:
> I do not wish to hurt your feelings at this time and I am most sorry for having caused you any past grief. You know that I am facing death. I am a wretched sinner but I believe in the salvation of Jesus Christ, our Lord. I want to try to reconcile any differences between others and myself in so far as I am able. Please do not be bitter against me. You trust in God and he will bless you if you do not hate anyone. Of course, you have a very good cause to be indignant against crime. However, I hope you will not hinder your harmony with God by bitterness.
> I am writing this letter from a purely Christian standpoint. I do not hold anything against anybody. I wish you joy and happiness. . . . God loves us all. I have opened my heart to him. I repent and praise Jesus for my deliverance. I hope everybody will love and serve God so that all violence and injury will cease. I do not ask any favor for my

own self. I ask you to pray for us condemned men here at San Quentin for the glory and in the name of our Lord.

I believe Mr. Toms is living in the spirit of Christ and you can meet him in Heaven. Life is eternal through the Son of God.

A contrite and humble sinner,

W. E. Hickman

Hickman also wrote to a police chief in Fort Worth, Texas, admitting to having robbed a cafeteria and a pharmacy there in December 1926. He wrote to another law enforcement official in San Francisco and confessed to several robberies during that same month and to some that occurred in January 1927. He also sent similar confessional letters to cities in Kansas, Oklahoma, Ohio, and Missouri. In each letter, he introduced himself as "William Edward Hickman, the killer of Marion Parker." He felt that it was his official title—his claim to fame as it were. With it, he achieved status and notoriety, an infamy that his exploits as a high school orator had never afforded him. He had long considered himself a "master crook." This act seemed to validate such a lofty opinion.

Hickman did neglect to apologize to the Parker family. He did not express remorse in writing for his greatest crime. Instead, he exploited it as if it were a part of his signature. Hickman even admitted to reporters that he should never have taken on an insanity defense. He stated that he should have "stood up like a man and made my peace with God." This was a real hindrance to Walsh and Cantillon's continued efforts to keep Hickman from the gallows.

In a written statement for the newspapers, Hickman stated, in part,

> Crime and other evils are signs of ignorance and death. All criminals and unrighteous men are struggling in the clutch of satanic error. By willful disobedience to God's law they become ignorant of the laws of truth and life.
>
> All creation is based upon positive force. Such is the will of God. However the devil is exerting his influence upon the minds of men in order to tear down the work of God.
>
> The reason that I became such a horrible criminal was because I allowed a demon of hell to lead me on. I praise God for lifting me up out of the pit of darkness and corruption.
>
> I beg young people to keep a close watch over their morals. Cling to the Christian faith and practice.

May God bless the people of the United States.[2]

As the days went by and the date of Hickman's execution drew closer, he received a handful of visitors. One of them was Welby Hunt, who had been sentenced to spend life in prison for the murder of Ivy Thoms. Hunt pleaded with Hickman to do something for him now that Edward was about to hang. Hickman refused. He knew that Hunt had killed Thoms despite what he told others. Hickman stated that he would help Hunt only if he could do so without lying. He asked Welby to embrace God. As he left Hickman, Hunt's face was crimson with anger.

Welby Hunt indeed served a long prison term, but it did not last his entire life. Welby Hunt was blessed with a particularly long time on this earth. After serving many years with good behavior, Hunt was finally released from prison on parole. He settled in the California area, working hard to escape the stigma of having served a prison term for murder. No longer interested in the crimes that had attracted him as a teenager, Welby Hunt had been completely rehabilitated in prison and as a grown man did not want any more trouble once released and on parole. He had experienced quite enough. Welby Hunt died in Rancho Mirage, California, on May 26, 1995, at the ripe old age of eighty-four. During those rare times when he would talk about his past, he would proclaim himself wholly innocent of the crime for which he spent most of his life behind bars. He always insisted that Hickman did it. Hickman was the master behind Hunt's apprenticeship. Hickman had murdered others and had killed and dismembered twelve-year-old Marion Parker. It was easy for Welby Hunt to pass the buck.

Perhaps the most surprising visit Hickman received during his final days on the planet was from his own father. William Thomas Hickman had deserted Edward as a child. He had all but disowned him initially on hearing of the Marion Parker murder. But he had had a change of heart and testified for the defense as to his son's insanity, offering important information about his wife's family background. It was a valiant try but was all for naught. This time, William Hickman Sr. arrived at San Quentin Prison to tell his son good-bye.

Bill Hickman was given permission to speak privately with Edward and stayed with him for nearly an hour. Reporters were waiting outside when the elder Hickman emerged from the prison building. He face was ashen, and he was crying.

"The boy is very brave. I thought I'd console him, but he consoled me instead. He said he loved the Parker girl and was sorry he killed her. He told me to live a Christian life and he'd see me in a little while. He gave me a message for his mother. I will give it to her and nobody else."[3]

Hickman also met with his defense lawyers, Jerome Walsh and Richard Cantillon, for the purpose of drawing up his last will and testament. He had little and left it all to his mother.

Just as the murder, manhunt, capture, and trial had overtaken the nation's papers, the press now printed nearly every detail leading up to Hickman's execution. There was tremendous speculation, but the most persistent rumor was that Perry Parker planned to attend the execution with his son. Parker remained silent for several weeks, trying to ignore the press accounts and get on with his life. He was tired of the hoopla surrounding his daughter's murder and wanted desperately to help his family heal emotionally from the tragedy. It was separation from the media hoopla they wanted most. Parker had figured that once the trial and sentencing were over, he would be left alone and could return to the peaceful anonymity that he and his family enjoyed until Marion's murder. But that was not to be.

The press remained persistent, and soon the rumors had become so strong that his friends and coworkers expected him to make the trip to San Quentin. Perry Parker tried to continue ignoring the rumors until finally he could be silent no more. Parker reluctantly called a press conference and made an official statement:[4]

"Certainly I'll not attend (the execution). Such reports are absurd. That is furthest removed from my mind. The execution means nothing to us except that the law is taking its course. We have no desire to be present; none whatever. In the execution we recognize only one more link in that inevitable chain of events that must be wielded before we can forget. Since the trial we have had only one desire: to have it all over with, so that we can begin healing from our wounds and forgetting our loss. Removal of this man is necessary to that end. When he is gone, when he is dead, there will be that much less left to bring back to us the memory of what we have lost and what we have suffered."

Now, perhaps, they would leave him and his family alone.

Perry W. Parker, Marion's brother, stated that he also had no plans to attend.

Perry Parker's life had once been quiet and pleasant. The Parkers were a happy family whose tranquillity was viciously rocked by the worst possible tragedy. Perry Parker was tired—tired of the police, the press, the trial, and the well-meaning public. He was tired of strangers recognizing him from his picture in the paper and offering consoling words. He realized that these people meant well, and he appreciated their concern. But it was over. Marion was not coming back. He simply wanted to wrap his arms around his surviving family members and move them away, emotionally, from the horror of Marion's murder. Perry Parker was asking for very little—just to return to the quiet, tranquil life he had enjoyed until that terrible day in December 1927.

The Parkers may have wanted to separate themselves from the tragedy, but they were not quite ready to completely let go. The train set that Marion had played with the day before her disappearance remained set up on the living room floor. And each afternoon, at the approximate time that Marion would normally arrive home from school, her dog still looked out the front window and cried.

CHAPTER 34

There was another rumor floating around. Word had hit the rumor mill that Eva Hickman was en route to see her son during his final days. The warden allowed time before the execution, indicating that he believed that the mother should have some final moments with her son if she was indeed making the trip to California. Eva Hickman never left home. It had all been merely a rumor that grew and eventually found its way into the press. But just to make sure, the warden waited until 9:00 p.m. the night before Hickman's execution before he took the killer to the death house.

William Edward Hickman had thirty-seven hours left on this earth. He was taken to the death house at 9:00 p.m., and that is where he would spend his final hours. His only request was a phonograph and a stack of records. Hickman had stated to the press that the two things he missed most in prison were listening to music and going to the movies. He was denied the right to attend the movies that were shown to prisoners, believing that his presence in the prison's general population was far too dangerous, even under guard. Hickman was unhappy to be forbidden from seeing favorite actress Esther Ralston in *Sawdust Paradise* or Buster Keaton in *The Cameraman* when these movies were screened for inmates. But he understood the safety issue. Hickman was allowed, during these final hours, to play some records. A phonograph and records were provided, ranging from classical music to popular recordings of the time. Hickman played all of them repeatedly but mostly the aria "Ave Maria," which he listened to intently with his eyes closed, his body slowly swaying back and forth to the music. It was as if this aria took him away from the very real situation he faced. It is unknown whether Marion's favorite song, *Pretty Baby*, was among the discs.

Hickman also wrote several more letters, including a note to one of his captors, Chief Tom Gurdane of Pendleton, Oregon. This is the same Chief Gurdane who returned to Oregon from California with a comparative pittance of reward money after he had been instrumental in nabbing the criminal whose escape prompted one of the largest nationwide manhunt's in the country's history. In his letter to Gurdane, Hickman apologized for pretending to insanity while incarcerated there. He equated this dodge as being just as ghastly as the murder of Marion Parker. Even in his alleged contrition, Hickman still felt the need to announce his greatest crime in every letter he wrote.

Also during these final hours, Hickman spent a great deal of time with Father William Fleming, who often visited prisoners just prior to their execution. While such a thing conjures up old movie images of the soft-spoken priest Pat O'Brien visiting contrite gangster James Cagney during his final moments in the 1938 Warner Bros. classic *Angels with Dirty Faces*, a Hollywood sequence such as this came years later and was, in fact, inspired by real events, such as the story of a murderer like William Edward Hickman. Father Fleming listened to Hickman's feelings about Jesus, about salvation, and about forgiveness.

"I'm not afraid anymore," Hickman told him. "I'm not afraid to die. I sent letters to everyone I could, asking their forgiveness and understanding. I spent many nights praying to God that He forgive me. I believe we will all meet in the hereafter."

Hickman indeed sent many letters, some to sheriffs and deputies from towns where he engaged in the pettiest of crimes. But he still had sent no letter to Perry Parker, and he continued announcing, with some fanfare, his crime of killing Marion Parker in every letter he wrote.

Before leaving Hickman, Father Fleming gave him Holy Communion. Hickman took great peace in the father's visit. Fleming would live another seven years and continued to make prison visits such as this to the very end of his days.

It was the night before the execution, and Hickman couldn't sleep. Neither could San Quentin Prison Warden James Holohan. The warden was fraught with a barrage of calls throughout the night, mostly from unstable women pleading with him to save Hickman's life. During these days of early celebrity, women often became attracted to the status of a young, attractive criminal. It would happen with John Dillinger, Pretty Boy Floyd, and other notorious gangsters of the Depression era, which was to occur only a few years later.

At one point during the night, Hickman called out to death house guard Charles Alston.[1]

"I want to talk to somebody," he said.

Alston slowly walked over to Hickman's cell and faced the notorious killer of Marion Parker and Ivy Thoms. Hickman had little time left, and it would seem that he had already told everything about the crime for which he was about to die.

The guard was a family man with children of his own. Two of them were daughters near Marion Parker's age. He despised Hickman and later admitted that it was difficult to resist the urge to spit in the convicted murderer's face. But he also realized that any final word from a prisoner about to die might be more revealing than that which had gone before. So he asked the only question that could possibly have been on his mind.

"Why did you kill Marion Parker?"

One would assume that Hickman had a pat answer to that question, having been asked so many times. But this time, Hickman just shrugged. The answer was even more pat and more flippant than the guard had imagined.

"Because I got tired of finding her in the room where I kept her while I was trying to get the ransom money. It got so that the sight of her face drove me into a frenzy."

Alston was nonplussed, incredulous. Questions rang inside his head. That was it? That's all? Hickman, in his final hours, admits that his sole reason for murdering this delightful little girl was simply because he was sick of looking at her?

After nearly a year's worth of headlines, a sensational trial, and a series of confessions that became more specific and more gruesome with each retelling, Hickman revealed, on his last night alive, that Marion Parker was killed because she had become an inconvenience. His grandiose plan of kidnapping for ransom had gone smoothly until the botched Friday night exchange. It wasn't smooth after that. Marion was a small child who wanted her mother and father. She was not to be consoled. She became an inconvenience.

There was no mention of Providence or of visions appearing before Hickman, egging him on and ordering him to murder. Marion was crying and carrying on, making demands to be returned home. He didn't want her there anymore. And he got her out of the way as if she was that much dust behind the couch.

"Why didn't you just drop her off in front of her house and leave the state?"

Hickman shuffled his feet a bit.

"It's funny you should say that. Marion said that same thing. I almost did it, but I thought she would scream and alert the police guards at the Parker home before I could make a clean getaway."

Feeling that he may be tapping into something, the guard challenged Hickman. "Why didn't you take her out on a side street or into the country and leave her?"

Hickman looked down and shook his head. He didn't answer right away. He sat on his bunk and thought for a moment. Then he looked up at the guard.

"That's where I used bad judgment," he admitted.

Hickman started to walk toward the guard as he continued to speak.

"I used bad judgment all the way through. I could have robbed a bank, got 10 times (more than the $1,500 ransom) and would have suffered far less serious consequences when captured."

As Hickman continued, he revealed his lofty opinion of himself once again. "I guess it was the most terrible crime in the history of the world," he said. And then added, "If ever a mortal deserved to be hanged, I do."

Charles Alston realized what Hickman wanted. He was about to die, and there was no turning back. The only shot he had at life was a last-minute reprieve from the governor, and that seemed impossible at this point. So, with eternity staring him in the face, Hickman wanted his final conversation on this earth to call the greatest attention to the one thing he accomplished that gave him the notoriety and infamy he had craved since entering his first oratory contest—William Edward Hickman, the master crook, the manipulator of the courts, and the man who killed and dismembered a little girl and became the most reviled creature in the nation. Everyone could not love Hickman. He came much closer to achieving worldwide hatred. And it was that sort of lofty status that he desired.

Hickman didn't brag when he was caught. He instead tried to pass himself off as another person. Just as District Attorney Asa Keyes had stated in court, Hickman's sanity was proven by his attempts to get away rather than brag about the crime. But now that he was caught and there was no way out, Hickman was ready to brag. He was declared sane by a court of law and was to be executed for a cold-blooded murder. It was that simple.

Hickman wasn't finished talking. His next comment effectively dismissed the many months of effort employed by his two defense attorneys.

"I wasn't crazy when I killed the Parker girl," he admitted. "I would have killed my best friend to get what I wanted."

Alston was ready to walk away. He didn't need to hear Hickman brag about this crime, even if his boasting included the understanding that he did, indeed, deserve the gallows.

But Hickman still wasn't finished. After admitting that he wasn't crazy, that he was, indeed, every bit the evil fiend that the prosecutors described, he looked up at the guard with a smirk. It was the same confident smirk he had shown Mrs. Mary Holt at Marion's school, the one that exuded such confidence and that helped convince Mrs. Holt to allow Marion to leave the building with the man who killed her only a couple of days later.

Alston didn't like Hickman's smirk. He was not impressed with his smugness.

Hickman continued smirking and looked directly into the guard's eyes.

"I got a kick out of dissecting Marion's corpse," he said.

The guard was shocked, and he seethed with anger. Boasting of the killing in a manner that led him to believe himself a "master crook" was bad enough. Hickman was now expressing enjoyment at his heinous act.

And with that, Hickman started to laugh. The guard walked away from the death house, Hickman's maniacal laughter ringing in his ears.

Alston wanted to kill Hickman right then and there. He wanted to reach into the cell and rip Hickman to shreds with his bare hands. He even later admitted to entertaining the idea of finishing Hickman off, making it look accidental, and somehow hoping public opinion would

not convict him of killing a man who had been proven guilty and responsible for killing and dismembering a twelve-year-old girl.

But he wisely waited for the state to take care of Edward Hickman's
expiration. And that was to occur in a mere eight hours.

CHAPTER 35

At 9:50 a.m. on Friday, October 19, 1928, Warden James Holohan and Father William Fleming visited William Edward Hickman in his cell.

It was time.

Hickman had consumed a breakfast of eggs, prunes, a roll, and coffee. Reporters, giving attention to any and every detail surrounding Hickman on this day, reported it as a small meal or a large meal, depending on which newspaper one was reading. Hickman was dressed handsomely in a new black suit as he accompanied Father Fleming and Warden Holohan down his proverbial last mile to the gallows. It wasn't a mile, of course, but the cliché was already in place at the time of Hickman's execution, and that is how it was reported in the press. Hickman had only about forty feet to walk before reaching his final destination on this earth.

Mobility was a problem for Hickman. His ankles were chained, and his arms were tied to his sides. There were two large, burly guards, one on either side of him. Well dressed and steady, Hickman did not, however, exude the confidence one finds in the cocky James Cagney movie character who defiantly threatens to spit in the eye of the guards. Hickman was once again meek little Edward. No bragging, no confidence, just another murderer whose life was about to end.

Hickman entered the courtroom saying the Litany with Father Fleming. There were a dozen witnesses, many of them journalists covering the event. As Hickman drew closer, the voices got louder. More than one spectator made an audible comment about the irony of child-killer Hickman reciting scripture.

The group approached the platform slowly. Hickman's confidence the night before, his cackling smugness as he announced how he "got a kick out of dissecting Marion's corpse," was no longer evident. He looked pale and nervous, and he stuttered over the Litany as he headed closer toward the gallows that were set to end his life in only a matter of minutes. Beads of sweat formed on his brow.

The group reached the platform. Hickman's foot was noticeably shaking as he lifted it onto the first of the thirteen steps that would be the last steps he would take. Roughly halfway up the stairs, Hickman's legs buckled, and he nearly fell into a faint. The two strong guards stationed on either side grabbed his arms. He was helped up the remaining five steps and now stood before the executioner. Hickman was visibly trembling as he faced the very end. He was not in the death house with eternity hours away. He was here, and the time for his execution was now. There would be no more boasting about dissecting a child's corpse.

Hickman was asked if he had anything to say.

He did not.

William Edward Hickman was finished talking. He had said everything he was going to say about the murder, his insanity ploy, and everything else. No more letters would be written proclaiming himself a "master criminal." And he was about to pay for accomplishing the "crime of the century." It seemed a fitting irony that William Edward Hickman, who took to boasting of his exploits during his final hours, had nothing to say as a final statement on this earth. Big talkers are often revealed to be cowards. Braggarts are often at a loss for words when confronted with cold, hard reality. And the reality was that Hickman was about to be just as dead as the innocent little girl he killed for becoming an inconvenience and whose corpse he said he took pleasure in dissecting.

The noose was placed around the trembling Hickman's neck. It was slowly tightened until it was snug. As the executioner stepped back, Hickman's legs buckled again; only this time, he fell into a faint.

The timing was perfect.

Just as Hickman was fainting, the executioner sprang the trap door beneath Edward's feet. Hickman's body went through, but because of his fainting, the action did not break his neck and cause instantaneous death, as was the standard. Because he was falling into a faint at the very second the trap was sprung, Hickman's body altered just enough for his weight to shift. Instead of being killed instantly, Hickman was, with even more alarming irony, being strangled to death by the noose, just as he strangled Marion Parker.

Hickman's bound body quivered and dangled, moving and flailing about as the rope slowly choked the life from him, just as he had done to Marion Parker. He gurgled and coughed, his body going into spasms as the oxygen was cut off from his lungs. There was a noise from below. One of the spectators fainted, his wooden chair toppling as he fell. Then another spectator fainted at the sight of the body dangling and flailing at the end of a rope. His wooden chair toppled as well. Some of the other reporters watched, some looked away, and others glanced between the struggling Hickman and their notepads, quickly scribbling every detail of Hickman's final struggle in life. There was another noise from the spectators. It was another person fainting, his chair also toppling onto the floor. Shortly after that, a fourth reporter fainted.

As security revived and removed each of these more squeamish on-lookers, Dr. Ralph Blecker edged closely to the dangling corpse. He put the stethoscope against its chest and listened for a heartbeat. He could not announce Hickman's death until the heart had stopped beating.

But the heart didn't stop beating, even after the body became steady. Marion Parker's heart had likely still been beating when her body went limp as Hickman strangled her. Her body had leaped from the Hickman's bathtub during his dissection of her corpse, just as her spine was cut. Even the doctor who performed the autopsy on Marion Parker stated that he could not determine if she had, indeed, died from the strangling or if death had happened later.

The death house guard waited at his post, listening for word of Hickman's demise. It was a longer time coming than he expected. Hickman's laughter kept ringing in his ears, along with the line "I got a kick out of dissecting Marion's corpse."

Time kept ticking away. Seconds had become minutes, and the minutes continued on. The body kept flailing and twitching after five minutes and then after ten.

Hickman had dropped through the trap door at 10:10 a.m. It was not until 10:25 a.m. that Dr. Ralph Blecker listened to Hickman's chest and heard nothing.

"Dead," he announced.

It had taken more than fifteen minutes for the hangman's noose to strangle William Edward Hickman, much less time than it took Marion Parker to pass out from the towel wrapped tightly around her neck. And it was still not fully determined if she even was dead when Hickman sliced apart her body.

Marion Parker did not deserve to die. She was a child who enjoyed life and harmed no one. Family, friends, and neighbors loved her. She was described in the press by those who knew her as cute, resourceful, playful, athletic, and happy and as having had a sense of humor and an abundance of enthusiasm.

William Edward Hickman was a frightened, angry, confused, ego-centric, petty thief and cold-blooded killer who ended the life of a little girl and dismembered her corpse. He later used this horrible act as an attention-getting ploy, even bragging about it as he apologized to other victims for lesser crimes. And, during his final hours as a living, breathing human being, he admitted to have taken pleasure in the dismemberment of the child's body. Despite the passionate arguments of William Edward Hickman's defense attorneys, on October 19, 1928, the reported conversation with guard Charles Alston is proof that a truly horrible person was put to death in the gallows at San Quentin Prison.

EPILOGUE

The Marion Parker murder was at the forefront of the nation's heart for several months. It found its way into the culture with folk songs devoted to the crime. Folk music was quite popular during this period and would remain so throughout the 1930s, with people like Woody Guthrie and Hughie "Leadbelly" Ledbetter among the most prominent artists. Folk songs reflected the times, the culture, and the news.

In the Negro spiritual church song "California Kidnapping," by Reverend J. M. Gates, he compares the case to his own family's past. He states that, like this California kidnapping, his "grandmother and grandfather were kidnapped out of the deepest darkest jungles of Africa. Bloodhounds chased them. Then Abraham Lincoln with stroke of a pen, freed po' Negroes and the half Negro men!"

Other folk songs included "The Fate of Edward Hickman," by Blind Andy, which was released just after the Hickman sentencing; "The Marion Parker Murder," by John McGhee, which came out in March 1928; and the decidedly prophetic "The Hanging of the Fox," by Vernon Dalhart, under the pseudonym Al Craven, which was released on April 5, 1928, a good six months before Hickman met his ultimate fate. The song "Little Marian Parker," another 1928 release, had these lyrics:[1]

> Way out in California, a family bright and gay
> Were planning for a Christmas not so very far away;
> They had a little daughter, a sweet and pretty child,
> And all the folks that knew her loved Marian Parker's smile.
> She left her home one morning for school not far away,

And no one dreamed that danger would come to her that day;
And then a murd'rous villain, a fiend with heart of stone,
Took little Marian Parker away from friends and home.
And then they caught the coward, young Edward was the man,
They brought him back to justice, his final trial to stand;
There is a grave commandment, it says thou shalt not kill,
And those who would not heed it, their cup of sorrow fill.
This song shall be a warning to parents far and near:
You cannot guard too closely the one we love so dear.

These folk songs were not top-level hits of the era and have not lived on except in the annals of American music historians. They did not receive a great deal of radio play outside of rural areas on stations that specialized in country folk. However, they were readily available in record shops, released by such national distributors as Columbia and Okeh. One wonders how the Parkers might have reacted to seeing their murdered child's name on a record label.

In 1928, writer Ayn Rand had plans for a novel, *The Little Street*, that featured a protagonist to be based on how she perceived William Edward Hickman. The book was never finished, but Rand's notes were published posthumously in *Journals of Ayn Rand*.[2] In these notes, Rand stated that the fascination with Hickman is due not to the crimes but to his "defiant attitude and his refusal to accept conventional morals." She describes him as "a brilliant, unusual, exceptional boy" and speculates about the society that turned him into "a purposeless monster." Rand wanted the protagonist of her novel to be "a Hickman with a purpose. And without the degeneracy. It is more exact to say that the model is not Hickman, but what Hickman suggested to me."

And what about the Parker family?

Once Hickman was dead, Perry Parker told the press that he was glad it was over and that he intended on continuing to help his family get back to normal. It was something that he had been trying to do since the trial. Now that full closure had come, Perry Parker wanted to move as far away from this horrible incident as he could. He would forever keep Marion in his heart and tried to no longer be haunted by the dismembered body that he held lifeless in his arms.

With the final articles on Hickman's execution already in the press, the Parkers eventually became yesterday's news. There would be new stories, new sensations, and other crimes to attract newspeople. The press stopped bothering Perry Parker, just as they would any celebrity who had outlasted his time in the spotlight. However, in Parker's case, the spotlight had never been welcome, nor had his perverse celebrity status. He never spoke to the press again.

Perry Parker lived another sixteen years, still mourning the loss of the daughter he loved so much, the child whose decapitated body he held in his arms, her face drained of life, peering through deadened eyes that had been stitched open by her killer. His passing in 1944 at the age of fifty-seven went by quietly and was barely noticed by the press that had once hovered over the story of his murdered little girl.

Geraldine Parker lived until 1963, when she died of cancer at the age of seventy-five. Although decades had separated her from her daughter's murder, the local California press did carry a story of her passing. The headline stated, "Mother of Kidnap Case Figure Dies," giving some cursory background to the murder of Marion Parker that had occurred more than thirty-five years earlier.

Geraldine had moved to the San Diego, California, area three years after Perry Parker's death, and at the time of her passing, she was living with her daughter Marjorie Parker Holmes and Marjorie's husband. Geraldine's son, Perry W. Parker, was, at this time, chief of plant protection and safety at the Northrop Corporation plant in Hawthorne, California. He had a daughter and two grandchildren.

In 1967, Richard Cantillon, one of Hickman's defense lawyers, died. But just before his death, he wrote a book about the case, but it did not see publication until five years later. His book, *In Defense of the Fox*, was published posthumously in 1972 by a smaller press and is now long out of print. It is one of the few books by an attorney that examines a case in which he failed to prove his client's innocence. Remarkably, Cantillon's book essentially sees Hickman as another victim, one who should have been allowed to live. Cantillon went to his grave still believing that his client, William Edward Hickman, was insane and wrongfully executed. At the conclusion of his book, the defense lawyer recalls how he visited Hickman just before his walk to the gallows and how he later shed bitter tears on the killer's execution. The book seemed to state that Cantillon blamed himself for Hickman's execution much the same way that Mary Holt blamed herself for allowing Marion to be taken from school by the stranger who later killed her. Unconfirmed reports indicate that Mrs. Holt ended up dying in a mental institution.

Asa Keyes, Hickman's chief prosecutor, had also been district attorney for the 1926 kidnapping case involving radio evangelist Aimee Semple McPherson. He achieved a rather lofty level of celebrity status from this and the Marion Parker case and was on the verge of becoming a household name. It was a status he enjoyed. It can be assumed that had he been around in the television age, he would likely have been a noted courtroom pundit.

But the public's respect for Keyes soon turned to shame. In 1929, a little more than a year after the Hickman trial, Keyes was on trial himself on charges of bribery. His distinguished career ended in disgrace. As a result, history has allowed him to achieve little notoriety in our collective memories.

Marion's older brother, Perry W. Parker, died on April 8, 1983, in Los Angeles, just three months shy of his seventy-sixth birthday. Marion Parker's twin sister, Marjorie Parker Holmes, had achieved her own level of infamy simply due to being the twin who was spared by the killer. Marjorie had been shielded from much of the media hoopla during the subsequent investigation and trial involving the man who murdered her sister. While the modern era would probably have netted her a massive book deal, there is no known record of her discussing Marion's kidnapping and murder at any time during her life. Marjorie Parker Holmes was still residing in the San Diego area when she passed away on August 2, 1987, at the age of seventy-one.

The killing of Marion Parker was, indeed, considered by many to be the most horrible crime this country had known, even overshadowing the notorious Leopold–Loeb murder of a young boy only a few years earlier. But in only five years, the killing of Marion Parker was itself overshadowed by the 1932 kidnapping and murder of famous aviator Charles Lindbergh's infant son. "Lucky Lindy" had been at the height of his aviator heroism back in 1927 at the time that Marion Parker was kidnapped and killed. During the press reports of the Lindbergh kidnapping, the Marion Parker case was referred to often. And while a killer did pay for this crime, there are still arguments in some quarters that the convicted and executed Bruno Hauptman was, in fact, innocent, just as Hickman's defense attorneys spent the rest of their lives believing their client to have been insane and that he had unjustly gone to the gallows.

As for Marion herself, there were intriguing reports as recently as the 1990s from people who lived in the house that the Parkers once occupied in Los Angeles, the same place where the train set that Marion had played with on the morning of her murder still remained set up on the living room floor months after her death and the same place where Marion's dog spent each day, for several months, continuing to look out the front window awaiting her return. The family then living in the old Parker home reportedly kept hearing strange noises throughout the house and said that some of these noises sounded like a child calling out. A few reports indicated that an actual séance was held. It was determined that the noises were coming from the ghost of Marion Parker, her friendly spirit occupying the house in which she once lived with her family.

After all these years, Marion Parker is still trying to find her way home.

NOTES

INTRODUCTION

1. Most newspaper accounts spelled Marion's first name "Marian," as that is the usual spelling for a girl with this name. However, Marion is the correct spelling. It was her father's middle name and was used with the same spelling as her first name.

CHAPTER 1

1. "Teacher Tells How Kidnapper Took Victim Away," *New York Times*, December 19, 1927.
2. "Teacher Tells How Kidnapper Took Victim Away," *New York Times*, December 19, 1927.

CHAPTER 2

1. Correspondence between Parker and the kidnapper, December 15–17, are quoted from the trial transcript (vol. 2, 586–98, 895–902; vol. 3, 1388–90, 1427–30). Also quoted in Richard Cantillon, *In Defense of the Fox* (Anderson, SC: Droke House/Hallux, 1972), and Michael Newton, *Stolen Away* (New York: Pocket Books, 2000).

CHAPTER 3

1. "Descriptions Broadcast of Girl and Abductor," *New York Times*, December 17, 1927.

2. "Parents Still Have Hope: Mr. and Mrs. Parker, Worn by Anxiety and Grief, Think Marian [*sic*] Will Return Safely," *Los Angeles Times*, December 17, 1927.

3. Correspondence between Parker and the kidnapper, December 15–17, are quoted from the trial transcript (vol. 2, 586–98, 895–902; Vol, 3, 1388–90, 1427–30). Also quoted in Richard Cantillon, *In Defense of the Fox* (Anderson, SC: Droke House/Hallux, 1972), and Michael Newton, *Stolen Away* (New York: Pocket Books, 2000).

4. "Abductors Kill Girl, Give Body to Father," *Los Angeles Times*, December 18, 1927.

CHAPTER 4

1. Events and dialogue recounted in "Abductors Kill Girl, Give Body to Father," *Los Angeles Times*, December 18, 1927.

CHAPTER 5

1. "This Fiend Must Not Escape," *Los Angeles Times*, December 20, 1927.

2. Michael Newton, *Stolen Away* (New York: Pocket Books, 2000).

3. "Child Slayer Clues Fail in Los Angeles," *Los Angeles Times*, December 20, 1927.

4. "Child Slayer Clues Fail in Los Angeles."

5. "Teacher Tells How Kidnapper Took Victim Away," *New York Times*, December 19, 1927.

6. "Family Bowed in Grief," *Los Angeles Times*, December 19, 1927.

7. "Family Bowed in Grief."

CHAPTER 6

1. A Latin term used by police that translates to "method of operation."

2. "Murder Charge Stuns Mother of Hickman," *Kansas City Star*, December 20, 1927.

3. "Fingerprints Name Bank Employee as Girl's Kidnapper," *New York Times*, December 20, 1927.

CHAPTER 8

1. "Los Angeles Killer Eludes All Pursuit," *Los Angeles Times*, December 21, 1927.

2. "Los Angeles Killer Eludes All Pursuit."

3. "Superintendent Issue Statement," *Los Angeles Times*, December 20, 1927.

CHAPTER 9

1. "Hickman Caught in Oregon, Confesses Kidnapping Girl, Says Another Killed Her," *Echo News*, December 22, 1927.

2. "Hickman Caught in Oregon, Confesses Kidnapping Girl, Says Another Killed Her."

3. "Mr. Parker Relieved," *New York Times*, December 22, 1927.

4. "Hickman Caught in Oregon, Confesses Kidnapping Girl, Says Another Killed Her."

CHAPTER 10

1. "Text of Hickman's Confession," *East Oregonian*, December 22, 1927.

2. "Text of Hickman's Confession."

3. "Text of Hickman's Confession."

4. "Child Slayer Clues Fail in Los Angeles," *Los Angeles Times*, December 20, 1927.

5. "Text of Hickman's Confession."

6. Richard Cantillon, *In Defense of the Fox* (Anderson, SC: Droke House/ Hallux, 1972).

7. Cantillon, *In Defense of the Fox*.

8. "Mr. Parker Relieved," *Los Angeles Times*, December 22, 1927.

CHAPTER 12

1. "Hickman Confession: Transcript of Signed, Handwritten Confession of the Murder of Marion Parker by William Edward Hickman 12-26-27." www.badgehistory.com/hickmanconfession.html, 549–62.

CHAPTER 13

1. "Hickman Confession: Transcript of Signed, Handwritten Confession of the Murder of Marion Parker by William Edward Hickman 12-26-27." www.badgehistory.com/hickmanconfession.html, 567–70.
2. "Movies Foster Crime, Canon Chase Charges," *New York Times*, January 1, 1928.
3. David Hayes and Brent Walker, *The Films of the Bowery Boys* (Secaucus, NJ: Citadel Press, 1984).

CHAPTER 14

1. Richard Cantillon, *In Defense of the Fox* (Anderson, SC: Droke House/ Hallux, 1972).
2. "Open Letter from Parker Girl's Coroner," *Los Angeles Times*, December 27, 1927.
3. "Chief Responds to Coroner's Letter," *Los Angeles Times*, December 27, 1927.

CHAPTER 15

1. "Hickman Indicated for Thoms Murder," *Los Angeles Times*, January 5, 1928.
2. "Hickman Admits Guilt to His Mother," *Kansas City Star*, January 8, 1928.
3. "Reverend Praises Work of Police. Declares Judges Too Lenient," *New York Times*, January 1, 1928.

CHAPTER 16

1. Richard Cantillon, *In Defense of the Fox* (Anderson, SC: Droke House/Hallux, 1972).

2. Cantillon, *In Defense of the Fox.*

CHAPTER 17

1. Richard Cantillon, *In Defense of the Fox* (Anderson, SC: Droke House/Hallux, 1972).

2. "Fellow Prisoners Threaten Hickman," *Los Angeles Times*, January 7, 1928.

3. Cantillon, *In Defense of the Fox.*

CHAPTER 18

1. Richard Cantillon, *In Defense of the Fox* (Anderson, SC: Droke House/Hallux, 1972).

CHAPTER 19

1. "Pretty Baby," a song written by Tony Jackson in 1912, was published in 1916, also crediting Gus Kahn and Egbert Van Alstyne.

2. Richard Cantillon, *In Defense of the Fox* (Anderson, SC: Droke House/Hallux, 1972).

CHAPTER 20

1. "Hickman Thinks He Will Hang," *Los Angeles Times*, January 25, 1928.

2. "Charges against Judge Hardy," *Los Angeles Times,* January 25, 1928.

3. "Charges against Judge Hardy."

CHAPTER 21

1. "Jury Selected. Tentatively Includes 3 Women," *Los Angeles Times*, January 27, 1928.

2. "Jury Selected."

3. Richard Cantillon, *In Defense of the Fox* (Anderson, SC: Droke House/Hallux, 1972).

4. "I Never Should Have Let Marion Go," *Los Angeles Times*, January 27, 1928.

5. Michael Newton, *Stolen Away* (New York: Pocket Books, 2000).

6. Newton, *Stolen Away*.

CHAPTER 22

1. The testimony of William Hickman, Edward's father, is taken from the court transcripts, vol. 2, 704–33.

CHAPTER 23

1. The testimony of Eva Hickman, Edward's mother, is taken from the court transcripts, vol. 2, 734–44.

CHAPTER 24

1. The deposition of Thomas Lewis is taken from the court transcripts, vol. 1, 61–84.

2. The testimony of James Parker is taken from the court transcripts, vol. 1, 458–60.

3. The testimony of Dr. Skoog is taken from the court transcripts, vol. 2, 807–88.

4. Richard Cantillon, *In Defense of the Fox* (Anderson, SC: Droke House/Hallux, 1972).

CHAPTER 25

1. The testimony of Dr. Skoog is taken from the court transcripts, vol. 2, 807–88.

CHAPTER 26

1. The summation of Forrest Murray is taken from the court transcripts, vol. 3, 1443–68.

CHAPTER 27

1. The summation of Jerome Walsh is taken from the court transcripts, vol. 3, 1469–96.

CHAPTER 28

1. The summation of Richard Cantillon is taken from the court transcripts, vol. 3, 1497–537.
2. Richard Cantillon, *In Defense of the Fox* (Anderson, SC: Droke House/ Hallux, 1972).

CHAPTER 29

1. The summation of Asa Keyes is taken from the court transcripts, vol. 3, 1538–74.
2. Judge Trabucco's address to the jury is taken from the court transcripts, vol. 3, 1577–86.

CHAPTER 31

1. Jerome Walsh's motion for a new trial is taken from the court transcripts, vol. 3, 1590–93.

2. Judge Trabucco's sentencing is taken from the court transcripts, vol. 3, 1611–12.

CHAPTER 32

1. Leo G. Stanley, *Men at Their Worst* (New York: Appleton-Century, 1940).

CHAPTER 33

1. "Hickman Writes to Slain Man's Widow," *Los Angeles Times*, October 17, 1928.

2. Syndicated in several newspapers across the country.

3. "Hickman Visited by His Father," *Los Angeles Times*, October 28, 1928.

4. "Parker Will Not Attend Execution," *Illustrated News*, October 17, 1928.

CHAPTER 34

1. Michael Newton, *Stolen Away* (New York: Pocket Books, 2000).

EPILOGUE

1. Carson J. Robison, "Little Marian Parker," recorded in 1928 by Vernon Dalhart.

2. Ayn Rand, *Journals of Ayn Rand*, edited by David Harriman (New York: Dutton, 1997).

BIBLIOGRAPHY

BOOKS

Cantillon, Richard. *In Defense of the Fox*. Anderson, SC: Droke House/Hallux, 1972.

Flowers, R. Barri. *Murder of the Banker's Daughter*. Amazon Digital Services, 2014.

Hayes, David, and Brent Walker. *The Films of the Bowery Boys*. Secaucus, NJ: Citadel Press, 1984.

Newton, Michael. *Stolen Away*. New York: Pocket Books, 2000.

Ralston, Esther. *Some Day We'll Laugh*. Metuchen NJ: Scarecrow Press, 1985.

Rand, Ayn. *Journals of Ayn Rand*. Edited by David Harriman. New York: Dutton, 1997.

Russell, Tony, and Bob Pinson. *Country Music Records: A Discography*. New York: Oxford University Press, 2008.

Stanley, Leo G. *Men at their Worst*. New York: Appleton-Century, 1940.

ARTICLES

"Abductors Kill Girl, Give Body to Father." *Los Angeles Times*, December 18, 1927.

"Charges against Judge Hardy." *Los Angeles Times*, January 25, 1928.

"Chief Responds to Coroner's Letter." *Los Angeles Times*, December 27, 1927.

"Child Slayer Clues Fail in Los Angeles." *Los Angeles Times*, December 20, 1927.

"Clues to Cramer." *Portland Oregonian*, December 22, 1927.

Correspondence between Parker and the kidnapper, December 15–17, are quoted from the trial transcript (vol. 2, 586–98, 895–902; vol. 3, 1388–90, 1427–30).

"Descriptions Broadcast of Girl and Abductor." *New York Times*, December 17, 1927.

"Family Bowed in Grief." *Los Angeles Times*, December 19, 1927.

"Fellow Prisoners Threaten Hickman." *Los Angeles Times*, January 7, 1928.

"Find Hickman Sane, Guilty of Murder." *New York Times*, February 10, 1928.

"Fingerprints Name Bank Employee as Girl's Kidnapper." *New York Times*, December 20, 1927.

"Five Times Held as Girl Slayer." *Los Angeles Times*, December 21, 1927.

"Girl's Grisly Killing Had City Residents Up in Arms." *Metro News: LA Then and Now*, February 4, 2001.

"Hickman Admits Guilt to His Mother." *Kansas City Star*, January 8, 1928.

"Hickman Caught in Oregon, Confesses Kidnapping Girl, Says Another Killed Her." *Echo News*, December 22 1927.
"Hickman Faces Trial Judge." *Davenport Democrat*, January 25, 1928.
"Hickman Indicated for Thoms Murder." *Los Angeles Times*, January 5, 1928.
"Hickman Is Guilty; To Be Sentenced Early Sunday." *Zanesville Signal*, February 10, 1928.
"Hickman Lawyers Plan Insanity Defense." *Los Angeles Times*, January 3, 1928.
"Hickman Thinks He Will Hang." *Los Angeles Times*, January 25, 1928.
"Hickman Writes to Slain Man's Widow." *Los Angeles Times*, October 17, 1928.
"I Never Should Have Let Marion Go." *Los Angeles Times*, January 27, 1928.
"Jury Selected. Tentatively Includes 3 Women." *Los Angeles Times*, January 27, 1928.
"Let Murderers Hang." *Los Angeles Times*, December 21, 1927.
"Los Angeles Killer Eludes All Pursuit." *Los Angeles Times*, December 21, 1927.
"Movies Foster Crime, Canon Chase Charges." *The New York Times*, January 1, 1928.
"Mr. Parker Relieved." *Los Angeles Times*, December 22, 1927.
"Murder Charge Stuns Mother of Hickman." *Kansas City Star*, December 20, 1927.
"Mutilated and Lifeless Body of Kidnapped Girl Returned to Father for $1,500 Ransom." *Harve Daily News-Promoter*, December 18, 1927.
"Open Letter from Parker Girl's Coroner." *Los Angeles Times*, December 27, 1927.
"Parents Still Have Hope: Mr. and Mrs. Parker, Worn by Anxiety and Grief, Think Marian [sic] Will Return Safely." *Los Angeles Times*, December 17, 1927.
"Parker Will Not Attend Execution." *Illustrated News*, October 17, 1928.
"Reverend Praises Work of Police. Declares Judges Too Lenient." *New York Times*, January 1, 1928.
"Teacher Tells How Kidnapper Took Victim Away." *New York Times*, December 19, 1927.
"Text of Hickman's Confession." *Pendleton East Oregonian*, December 22, 1927.
"This Fiend Must Not Escape." *Los Angeles Times*, December 20, 1927.

SONGS

"Ave Maria," also known as "Ellens dritter Gesang" ("Ellens Gesang III," D. 839, Op. 52, No. 6), composed by Franz Schubert in 1825.
"California Kidnapping" written by Reverend J. M. Gates, 1929.
"Fate of Edward Hickman" written by Blind Andy, 1928.
"The Hanging of the Fox" written by Vernon Dalhart, 1928.
"Little Marian Parker" by Carson J Robison. Recorded in 1928 by Vernon Dalhart.
"The Marion Parker Murder" written by John McGhee, 1928.
"Pretty Baby" written by Tony Jackson in 1912, published in 1916 and also crediting Gus Kahn and Egbert Van Alstyne.

FILM

The March of Crime. Second edition (1936) Roadshow Attractions (States Rights Systems).

ONLINE

Gado, Mark. "My Baby Is Missing!" www.crimelibrary.com/criminal_mind/psychology/child_abduction/6.html?sect=19
Gribben, Mark. "The Murder of Marion Parker." http://malefactorsregister.com/wp/?p=779

"Hickman Confession: Transcript of Signed, Handwritten Confession of the Murder of Marion Parker by William Edward Hickman 12-26-27." www.badgehistory.com/hickmanconfession.html

Hillman, Bill. "Edgar Rice Burroughs Reports on the Notorious 1928 Hickman Trial." www.erbzine.com/mag17/1767.html

Welton, Benjamin. "Fox or 'Moral Imbecile'? William Edward Hickman and the Murder of Marion Parker." www.crimemagazine.com/fox-or-"moral-imbecile"-william-edward-hickman-and-murder-marion-parker

ALSO

Internet Movie Database
Murderpedia
Wikipedia
Note: Information from the court transcripts is also used as found in various newspaper articles and the books by Newton and Cantillon listed herein.

INDEX

ABOUT THE AUTHOR

James L. Neibaur is a film historian and educator who has published over fifteen books and written hundreds of articles, including more than forty essays in the *Encyclopedia Britannica*. His books include *The Fall of Buster Keaton*, *Chaplin at Keystone*, *The Silent Films of Harry Langdon*, and *The Charley Chase Talkies*.